18.22

GREAT MYSTERIES

The End of the World

OPPOSING VIEWPOINTS®

Look for these and other exciting *Great Mysteries: Opposing Viewpoints* books:

Alternative Healing
Amelia Earhart
Anastasia, Czarina or Fake?
Animal Communication
Artificial Intelligence
The Assassination of Abraham Lincoln
The Assassination of President Kennedy
Astrology
Atlantis
The Beginning of Language
The Bermuda Triangle
Bigfoot
Custer's Last Stand
The Devil
Dinosaurs
The Discovery of America
El Dorado, Land of Gold
The End of the World
ESP
Evolution
Jack the Ripper
King Arthur

Life After Death
Living in Space
The Loch Ness Monster
The Lost Colony of Roanoke
Miracles
Mysteries of the Moon
Noah's Ark
Pearl Harbor
Poltergeists
President Truman and the Atomic Bomb
Pyramids
Reincarnation
Relativity
Shamans
The Shroud of Turin
The Solar System
Stonehenge
The Trojan War
UFOs
Unicorns
Vampires
Voodoo

GREAT MYSTERIES
The End of the World
OPPOSING VIEWPOINTS®

by Michael Arvey

Greenhaven Press, Inc.   P.O. Box 289009, San Diego, California 92198-9009

Library of Congress Cataloging-in-Publication Data

Arvey, Michael.
    The end of the world : opposing viewpoints / by Michael Arvey.
       p. cm. — (Great mysteries)
    Includes bibliographical references and index.
    Summary: Explores different theories about how the world might end, including such possibilities as an extraterrestrial calamity, an environmental disaster, or a mystical apocalypse.
    ISBN 0-89908-096-0 (alk. paper)
    1. End of the world—Juvenile literature.   [1. End of the world.] I. Title. II. Series: Great mysteries
BLl503.A78 1992
001.9—dc20   92-15101
                                             CIP
                                             AC

To Dolly, Rich, and Bill

Contents

Introduction

This book is written for the curious—those who want to explore the mysteries that are everywhere. To be human is to be constantly surrounded by wonderment. How do birds fly? Are ghosts real? Can animals and people communicate? Was King Arthur a real person or a myth? Why did Amelia Earhart disappear? Did history really happen the way we think it did? Where did the world come from? Where is it going?

Great Mysteries: Opposing Viewpoints books are intended to offer the reader an opportunity to explore some of the many mysteries that both trouble and intrigue us. For the span of each book, we want the reader to feel that he or she is a scientist investigating the extinction of the dinosaurs, an archaeologist searching for clues to the origin of the great Egyptian pyramids, a psychic detective testing the existence of ESP.

One thing all mysteries have in common is that there is no ready answer. Often there are *many* answers but none on which even the majority of authorities agrees. *Great Mysteries: Opposing Viewpoints* books introduce the intriguing views of the experts, allowing the reader to participate in their explorations, their theories, and their disagreements as they try to explain the mysteries of our world.

But most readers won't want to stop here. These *Great Mysteries: Opposing Viewpoints* aim to stimulate the reader's curiosity. Although truth is often impossible to discover, the search is fascinating. It is up to the reader to examine the evidence, to decide whether the answer is there—or to explore further.

"Penetrating so many secrets, we cease to believe in the unknowable. But there it sits nevertheless, calmly licking its chops."

H.L. Mencken, American essayist

One

Is the End of the World Near?

Be prepared—the end of the world is coming! It will probably happen in this decade, before the year 2000, according to people who believe the end of a millennium, a period of one thousand years, will coincide with the end of the world. Historically, the end of a millennium—or even of a century—is a popular time for people to predict doomsday, the end of the world.

A.D. 1000

When the year 1000 approached, Europeans were filled with dread. Many believed that Armageddon would occur at the end of the millennium. In the Bible, the Book of Revelation describes this final battle between good and evil: "And when the thousand years are expired, Satan shall be loosed out of his prison, and shall go out and deceive the nations." Some believed Armageddon and the Second Coming of Christ would occur on Christmas Eve 999. Others believed these events would happen on December 31. Many interpreters elaborated on what the Bible said. Richard Erdoes, in his book *A.D. 1000*, described one person's vision "of the sky splitting open, letting fall down to earth a gigantic torch. . . . The shape of [a] dragon with blue feet appeared, its head continuing to grow

In this sixteenth-century painting, Dutch artist Pieter Brueghel depicts the two sides of the Last Judgment. Angels lead orderly rows of the "saved" off to heaven, while monstrous demons attack the panicking damned and hurl them into the mouth of a great sea serpent.

until it filled the horizon from end to end." In fact, a meteor appeared in September 999 over England, and people were afraid. "Whether this light came from God or from the devil people did not know," says Erdoes.

Other horrors also alarmed people. During the tenth century, wars had devastated the fields and farms throughout Europe. Famine was rampant. A commentator of the time named Glaber wrote that the people "believed that the orderly laws of nature had been suspended, that the natural flow of the seasons, which until then had ruled the earth, had fallen into utter disorder foretelling the end of all." According to Erdoes, conditions were so bad that starving people had resorted to cannibalism. He writes, "Parents ate their children. Robbers not only waylaid hapless travelers, but also devoured them."

Epidemics followed the famines and wars. Glaber wrote of a horrible plague that swept across Europe. The people had no effective medicines to stop it.

This catalog of distresses made many people believe that the world was indeed ending. At the close of the year 999, the old basilica of Saint Peter's in Rome filled with frightened worshipers waiting for the end that did not come. In the book *The Fringes of Reason*, Stanley Young comments, "All of Christendom threw a party—but Christ never showed up."

Although the end of a millennium is a popular time for predicting doomsday, predictions have been made for many other times as well. Young states, "People have always pondered the end,

Human corpses litter a medieval street during a plague. People often fear that such widespread disasters signal the end of the world.

since the very beginning. Throughout history prophets [have appeared] to preach doom and gloom, mass movements [have formed] proclaiming the . . . demise of the planet, groups of believers [have gone] up to mountaintops to wait out the earthquake/flood/fire/celestial collision/whatever." Fortunately, he points out, so far, no one has been right.

But many cultures disagree and believe that at some time in the distant past, the world did end— maybe more than once. Doomsday myths are found in literature from ancient India, Mesopotamia, Persia, Greece, Asia, and the Americas.

Has the World Ended Before?

To people of Western cultures, perhaps the best-known story of the world's ending is the story of Noah and the Flood. The Old Testament of the Bible contains this account in the Book of Genesis.

Noah, his family, and pairs of animals leave the ark that saved them from the great flood.

The story describes a world that has become decadent, full of sin and crime. God becomes displeased with the way humans have corrupted the perfect world he created. He tells Noah, one of the few good and just people left on earth, that in a short time, he will destroy the earth with a great flood. Only Noah and those creatures he brings aboard a hand-built ship will be saved.

Under God's direction, Noah builds his ship, the ark. Noah tries to warn people of the impending disaster, but they ignore or ridicule him. Finally, just as God's terrible rain begins to fall, the ark is finished. Noah ushers aboard the ship his wife and children and two of every kind of beast that inhabits the earth. Torrential rains fall for forty days and nights. All forms of life on earth, except for those on the ark, are destroyed. After forty days and nights, the waters begin to recede, and Noah's ark lands on the tip of Mount Ararat, believed to be in the Middle East. Noah and his family and the beasts he saved begin to repopulate the earth.

Flood Stories Come from Many Cultures

Similar stories are known throughout the world. For example, science writer Fred Warshofsky states in *Doomsday: The Science of Catastrophe* that members of many different South American Indian communities described a great flood "to the priests accompanying the conquering Spaniards." The Indians spoke of a people called Ancasmarca, named after a mountain in the Andes. A shepherd and his six sons and daughters had been warned by their llamas of a coming flood. Consequently, they gathered all the food and livestock they could and took it with them to the top of the mountain. When the flood came, it reached nearly to where the shepherd and his children were. After the flood receded, they repopulated the land of Ancasmarca.

Ancient Hindu writings tell of previous world ages called *yugas*. According to tradition, each yuga

"The flood legends that have come down to us . . . are a convincing indication that the human race in all parts of the world remembered a time of great flooding and destruction."

Charles Berlitz, *Doomsday: 1999 A.D.*

"No responsible scientist believes that there were worldwide catastrophes on the level of the universal deluge."

Daniel Cohen, *Waiting for the Apocalypse*

The sixth-century B.C. Persian prophet Zarathustra, or Zoroaster, described great cataclysms that ended the world in previous ages.

ended with a huge disaster. The sacred book *Bhagavata Purana*, for example, tells of former ages in which nearly all the people perished through catastrophic fires, floods, or hurricanes. Charles Berlitz, author of *Doomsday: 1999 A.D.*, reports that many Hindus believe the current age of humanity, the Kali Yuga, is drawing to a close. Soon it, too, will end in a terrible disaster.

The teachings of an ancient Persian religion called Mazdaism also referred to tremendous cataclysms that ended human civilization. Mazdaism's prophet, Zarathustra, told of "the signs, wonders, and perplexity which are manifested in the world at the end of each millennium." One disaster Zarathustra described was a great meteor that crashed into the earth, killing all life.

The late Russian-born psychiatrist and doomsday writer Immanuel Velikovsky described the beliefs of several ancient civilizations in his book *Worlds in Collision*. He wrote that the early Chinese believed humanity cycles through ages called *kis*, or convulsions of nature. Velikovsky referred to an ancient Chinese encyclopedia, *Sing-li-ta-tsuien-chou*, that said at the end of each kis, "the sea is carried out of its bed, mountains spring out of the ground, rivers change their course, human beings and everything are ruined."

Regular Cycles of Destruction

Ancient Greeks had their catastrophes, too. According to Velikovsky, Heracleitus, a philosopher from the sixth century B.C., "taught that the world is destroyed by fire every 10,800 years." Another Greek historian, Hesiod, described four ages that were destroyed by the wrath of the gods.

Velikovsky also noted that "an old tradition, and a very persistent one, of world ages that went down in . . . catastrophes . . . [is] found in the Americas among the Incas, the Aztecs, and the Mayas. A major part of the stone inscriptions found in Yucatan [in Mexico] refer to world catastrophes." These ancient civilizations believed the world had passed through four ages. Velikovsky cited a Mexican historical chronicle that said, "The ancients knew that before the present sky and earth were formed, [people were] already created and life had [begun] itself four times."

In North America, the Hopi tradition also incorporates the belief that the world has had four ages since its creation. Each age ended when the Creator destroyed human civilization because it was not living in harmony with nature and because the people were wicked. The Hopi believe the first age was destroyed by volcanoes; the second ended when the earth flipped over, end to end; and the third age was destroyed by great floods. The fourth age is the present one and the Hopi believe it could end soon.

Could these disasters the ancient speak of happen again? Many doomsday prophets think so.

Doomsday Movements

Doomsday prophets can generally be grouped into one of two categories: the religious or mystical prophets and the scientific. Religious or mystical prophets generally receive a revelation from a supernatural source telling them that doomsday is near. The source might be God, a sacred writing, or a visit from an extraterrestrial being, for example. Prophets of the scientific type usually determine, in what they think is a rational way, that present events are leading inevitably to the end of the world. For example, they might tally up the amount of pollution in the world and the destruction it is causing and conclude that the earth can only take so much more before it is totally destroyed. Often, doomsday prophets are so persuasive or charismatic that they attract many followers. Sometimes, these followers become united into a movement.

Typically, doomsday movements gain force when a prophet predicts the coming of some vital

"The beginning of the end of the present . . . world is considered by the Hopi to have already started and will be [finished] after the appearance of a now invisible star, rushing toward Earth from space."

Charles Berlitz, *Doomsday: 1999 A.D.*

"There is something dramatic and exciting about the vision of Venus flying at us and stopping the Earth's rotation. The fact that it is in defiance of all the laws of celestial mechanics is not something that would disturb the kind of person who is excited by such tales."

Isaac Asimov, *A Choice of Catastrophes*

future event. The event might be a great disaster, such as an earthquake that will drop California into the sea, or a great nuclear war. It might be the Second Coming of Christ, an event awaited by many religious groups for most of the past two thousand years. It might be the ominous visit to the earth by extraterrestrials. In some cases, the prophet tells of a way a select group of people will be saved from the mass destruction the rest of the earth will suffer.

The Millerites

Once such a prediction is made and has captured the imagination of a sizable group of people, a movement forms and group members work toward the goal of saving themselves or saving the world. One example of a doomsday movement is that formed by the Millerites, a group of religious doomsday believers in the early nineteenth century.

In 1818, New York farmer and fundamentalist Protestant William Miller began an ardent two-year study of the Bible. His study led him to conclude that the world would end and Christ would return in 1843. Miller began preaching his beliefs and little by little developed a band of followers. He believed the great event would occur on March 21, 1843. He and his followers prepared themselves to meet God. They waited together in Boston on March 21, but nothing happened. Miller returned to his calculations and said he had made a mistake. The real date should be March 21, 1844.

Again, his followers awaited the Second Coming with him. Again, it did not happen. Miller proposed a third date to his still faithful flock. It would happen on October 22, 1844 he said. But on that day, too, Christ failed to appear. The Millerites, as they were called, largely disbanded as a result of Miller's failed predictions. But some members evolved into the present-day Jehovah's Witnesses. In the past 150 years, this group has made three ad-

Doomsday prophet William Miller predicted the world would end in 1843, then 1844. For many of his followers, Miller's credibility ended when the world did not.

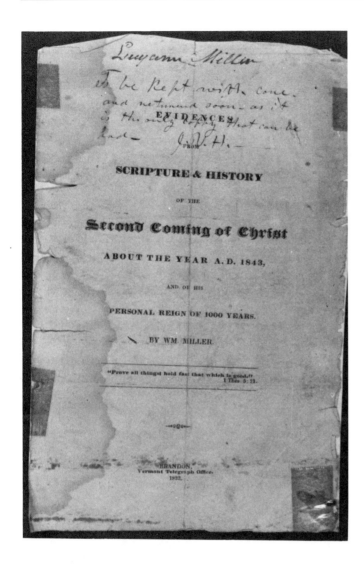

The title page from William Miller's book describing the biblical and historical basis for his prediction that Christ would return in 1843.

ditional predictions of the imminent end of the world—1874, 1914, and 1975. So far, their predictions have been wrong.

Other Modern Doomsday Movements

Another doomsday movement developed in 1910. It did not revolve around a particular prophet but around an event. In 1910, scientists knew that Halley's comet was due to appear, as it does every seventy-six years. A group of scientists predicted that the earth would move through the comet's tail and that poisonous gases from the comet would kill all life on earth. The newspapers played up the story, and millions of people panicked. Others took advantage of the situation. Daniel Cohen, author of *Waiting for the Apocalypse*, comments:

> [The coming of Halley's comet] inspired a rash of wild predictions. The comet, it was said, was going to collide with the earth and perhaps smash our puny earth to pieces. . . . There was . . . a real possibility that the earth would pass through the gaseous tail of the comet. . . . One enterprising Englishman took to selling comet pills—a harmless mixture of aspirin and sugar—to protect others from the effect of the poisonous gases.

As it turned out, the comet passed and nothing happened.

A recent doomsday movement revolved around the predictions of Elizabeth Clare Prophet, leader of the Church Universal and Triumphant. Prophet claims to be able to see the future. She declares that

A family group gathers in a prayer circle to await the world-ending Second Coming of Christ, which they believe is imminent.

huge natural disasters or even a nuclear war might destroy the planet. In 1989, she predicted that a nuclear war would occur within the coming decade, destroying most of the world. She and a group of her followers in Montana dug bomb shelters and stockpiled food. So far the war has not occurred as predicted.

A New World

Not every doomsayer believes the planet will be destroyed. But most do believe that a new world, or at least a new civilization, will replace the present one. In other words, a calamity will happen, and what survives of the world will be transformed in a dramatic way. José Argüelles, author of *The Mayan Factor*, believes that 2012 will be the year the world changes. He says the ancient Mayan calendar shows that in 2012, the world will complete its present cycle of spiritual ignorance and enter a heavenlike age. Dick Teresi and Judith Hooper, in *Omni* magazine, describe Argüelles's vision: "We'll live harmoniously . . . in New Age villages—equipped with 'solar temples,' lush gardens, . . . and 'houses of information.'"

Writer Richard Erdoes sums up the current doomsday prophecies: "It is no longer only the sandal-clad hermits and oddballs walking the streets . . . proclaiming 'the end of the world.' . . . Perfectly sane people, among them scientists and Nobel Laureates, predict humankind's demise due to overpopulation, pollution, depletion of the earth's ozone layer. . . . The end of Christianity's second millennium is near, and A.D. 2000 is just a few years away."

"Self-proclaimed prophets, for the most part, prey upon [human] need, often in their own self-interest."

Charles J. Cazeau, *The Skeptical Inquirer*, Winter 1990

"Perhaps the world really is going to end, or perhaps the ancient vocabulary of apocalypse is simply the handiest way to express the anxieties provoked by . . . rapid cultural change."

Dick Teresi and Judith Hooper, *Omni*, January 1990

Two

Do Religious Prophets Know When the End Will Come?

Since ancient times, some Christians have believed the world will end at some specified time and that good people will be reunited with their creator. This belief is emphasized by many passages in the Bible. In the Book of Matthew in the New Testament, for example, Jesus speaks of certain signs that will signal the end of the world. He says there will be wars and rumors of wars; nations will rise against nations; and famine, pestilence, and earthquakes will abound.

The Apocalypse

The Book of Revelation, also in the New Testament, presents a terrible vision of possible future events. Written by the apostle John two thousand years ago, it describes a long vision known as the Apocalypse—a dramatic and violent view of the end of the world followed by the reunion of the just with God. John describes a terrible battle, with angels and demons, disasters, monsters, and beasts. Ultimately, according to his vision, wickedness will be destroyed. But first, humanity will have to contend with many evils, including the Four Horsemen, who, some interpreters believe, represent four successive periods of woe for the world.

The First Horseman is the Messenger of Subju-

(Opposite page) The angels of heaven fight off the bat-winged minions of Satan. The scene, illustrated here by nineteenth-century artist Gustave Doré, is described in the Book of Revelation as part of the final conflict at the end of the world. Is this a myth or an accurate prediction?

gation. He rides a white steed, holds a bow, and wears a crown. John writes, "And he went out conquering and to conquer." J.R. Jochmans writes in his book *Rolling Thunder*, "The modern interpretation sees this rider as representing global imperialism [strong nations taking over weaker ones] by the Western powers [Europe and the United States] from 1881 until the early years of the twentieth century."

The Second Horseman is the Messenger of War. He rides a blood-colored horse and carries a large sword in order to "take peace away from the earth,

Famed fifteenth-century artist Albrecht Durer's rendition of the Four Horsemen of the Apocalypse: (left to right) Death, Famine, War, and Subjugation.

so that men should slay one another," John says. Jochmans points out that the Second Horseman may already have come. During the twentieth century, the world has experienced more wars than ever before. These include the Russo-Japanese War, the two world wars, the Vietnam War, the Northern Ireland conflict, the Six-Day War in the Middle East, the Persian Gulf War, and numerous other conflicts.

The Third Horseman is the Messenger of Famine. He rides a black horse and carries a pair of weight scales in his hands. Jochmans writes, "He represents the period many believe we have now entered. . . . John tells how during the times of this horseman, a handful of wheat and barley will cost a whole day's wages, . . . food and other essentials will be scarce, and prices will be greatly inflated." Each day, news reports describe places in the world where these things are true.

The Fourth Horseman rides a "deadly pale" horse and carries a sword. He is the Messenger of Destruction and Death. Jochmans says this is the most fearsome of all the horsemen. He signals a final global conflict. According to John's prediction, this horseman will be "given power over a fourth of the earth, to kill with a sword." Finally, after this horseman has done his work, there will be "a new heaven and new earth."

Armageddon and the Rapture

The Book of Revelation also describes hail and fire mixed with blood that will fall on the earth and destroy one-third of the vegetation. In addition, one-third of the ocean will turn to blood; a great earthquake will destroy all the cities in the world; one-third of humanity and everything in the sea will be destroyed; and the rivers and springs will become dry.

John's vision is horrific indeed, and it has captured the imagination of millions of Christians through the ages.

"Fundamentalist biblical literalism . . . [and its] vision of a young earth, with its surface and atmosphere almost entirely the product of the Deluge about 6,000 years ago, contradicts modern geological and astronomical science."

David Morrison and Clark R. Chapman, *The Skeptical Inquirer*, Winter 1990

"It appears that many of the old notions of Armageddon, the War in Heaven, and the creation and destruction of the world are even more plausible today than when they were first stated."

Dennis Stillings, *Utne Reader*, March/April 1990

Other biblical passages also describe great doomsday catastrophes. These include:

- tribulation, or hardship and distress, running rampant in the world seven years before the Second Coming of Christ;
- the death of the sun and the moon;
- the appearance of many false prophets claiming to be Christ;
- the arrival of the Antichrist—a person who will claim to be a savior but who will be "like a beast" and will try to enslave humanity;
- Armageddon, a final battle between good and evil forces;
- the Rapture—the return of Christ at the moment the world is on the verge of destruction. The Bible says Christ will appear in the sky, stop Armageddon, and physically whisk Christian believers, both dead and alive, up into the heavens.

Are the Prophecies True?

Stanley Young, writing in *The Fringes of Reason*, says that most Christians are cautious about believing John's predictions in Revelation. He states, "The original Church Fathers were wary of including Revelation in the Biblical canon at all." They feared "that its mystical signs and portents might be taken too literally. The fears of the Church Fathers have been continually borne out ever since." This is especially true in the last half of the twentieth century in the United States. Many fundamentalist Christians—those who emphasize literal interpretation of the Bible as the foundation for Christian life—believe the prophecies will happen just the way they are described in the Bible. Hal Lindsey is one of these Christians.

A former Campus Crusade for Christ staff member and author of *The Rapture* and other popular books, Lindsey believes the end is not far away. He writes, "All the predicted signs that set up the fi-

Since 1970, fundamentalist Christian author Hal Lindsey has written several books on the end of the world, which he believes is near.

In 1948, Israel's first prime minister, David Ben-Gurion (right of center, in jacket), bids farewell to British forces who had occupied Palestine since 1917. Some believe that Israel's return as a sovereign nation fulfills a biblical prophecy heralding the end of the world.

nal fateful period immediately preceding the Second Coming of Christ are now before us. Few people today doubt that history is moving toward some sort of climactic catastrophe." Lindsey and others believe that the 1948 founding of the nation of Israel is an important sign that the Second Coming is at hand. It was prophesied in the Bible as a sign of the impending Apocalypse.

Well-known evangelist Billy Graham also takes the warnings of Revelation seriously. In his book *Approaching Hoofbeats*, he writes, "John's four horsemen are already riding across the earth. They are ancient symbols of the modern terrors that pursue us: war, violence, deception, economic chaos, unemployment, poverty, hunger, disease, despair, and death." But Graham believes that rather than portending the end of the world, the horsemen are warnings that people must change their way of liv-

Renowned evangelist Billy Graham believes the Four Horsemen of the Apocalypse are riding through the world even now.

ing before it is too late. In other words, if people reform, they may be able to postpone—or even avoid—doomsday.

The Antichrist

Many Christian visions of doomsday include the prominent participation of the Antichrist, a person who claims to be humanity's savior but who is, in fact, the very antithesis of Christ. The Antichrist will be an evil being who will attempt to enslave humanity. Biblical references say he will oppose God and establish himself as an object of worship. He will fight those who are good and will dominate the world. Ultimately, however, he will be destroyed by the forces of God.

Some Christians believe that the Antichrist has already been on earth. For example, many people thought Adolf Hitler was the Antichrist. In Germany during World War II, Hitler was the leader of the totalitarian political and economic regime called

German Nazi leader Adolf Hitler tried to force the world to accept his master plan for humanity. Many people believed he was the Antichrist and that the world would end soon after he was defeated in World War II.

Nazism. Because of Hitler's policies, millions of Jewish people and others who did not conform to the Nazi ideals were captured, tortured, and killed. His diabolical actions led many to conclude that he must be the Antichrist.

Some believe the Antichrist is alive today, making this the last age before Armageddon. Three decades ago, American psychic Jeane Dixon claimed that the Antichrist was born on February 5, 1962, somewhere in the Middle East. She predicted that he would present himself to the world in 1991 or 1992, claiming to be able to solve the world's problems. Dixon has predicted that this monster will be destroyed by God in 1999.

Doomsday's Time

Many doomsayers believe they know when doomsday, often called the Tribulation by Christians, will occur. In 1983, Christian writer Mary Stewart Relfe claimed she had received a divine revelation about the Tribulation. She envisioned a coming World War III, which would result in the "partial destruction of the U.S. due to nuclear attack," according to William Alnor, author of *Soothsayers of the Second Advent*. (The *Second Advent* is another term for the Second Coming.) Relfe claimed the war would happen in 1989. It would be followed by the Tribulation in 1990 and the Second Coming in 1997. So far, Relfe has been wrong in her predictions.

Reginald Dunlop is another prophet who believed he knew doomsday's date. In 1977, he stated emphatically that by 1986, the world would be undergoing "worldwide famine" and that "the United States would feel hunger pains for the first time." He also stated that the Antichrist would be revealed in 1989 or 1990 and that the Rapture would start in 1991. Dunlop claimed that his information came directly from God. "I am *More* than positive that this is *The Year* that the Rapture will occur," he stated.

Two members of the Southwest Radio Church

American psychic Jeane Dixon claimed in 1962 that the Antichrist had been born on February 5th of that year in the Middle East. She predicted he would make himself known in 1992.

"The time is near. The End is at hand. This is the message that all millennial movements feed upon."

Stanley Young, *The Fringes of Reason*

"Responsible prophecy teachers need to make a pact to carefully investigate all prophecy statements. . . . The ministries spreading dangerous, false rumors about the end times must be stopped."

William Alnor, *Soothsayers of the Second Advent*

in Texas named David Webber and Noah Hutchings wrote the book *Prophecy in Stone*. The book contains a chart showing that the Tribulation should have begun between 1981 and 1985 and ended between 1989 and 1992. When the first dates came and went, the book went out of print. The authors, however, then revised their chart and came out with a new book called *Is This the Last Century?* The new book was a duplicate of the first one, with the exception of the chart. In the new version, they set the beginnning of the Tribulation in 1988 and Christ's coming in 1996. The authors claimed that the chart was made by a local pastor who later changed his mind about the dates.

Judging the Prophets

William Alnor believes the prophecies of people like Relfe, Dunlop, Webber, and Hutchings should not be taken seriously. They claim "to be a part of a small circle of His [God's] specially initiated people who can interpret prophecy." But so far, these people have been wrong. Prophets, Alnor argues, should be judged by their accuracy. "Their dedication may be admirable," he says of those who are devoted to watching the signs of the times for the church. "Their accuracy, however, is abysmal. They have made repeated grave errors in fact and judgment," Alnor says. He criticizes those Christians who use the Bible "as a fortune-telling" device to predict the future. He believes these people's inaccuracies have discredited God's word for many people.

Many so-called prophets simply try to guess the meaning of vague or mystical Scripture, says Alnor. "When we go beyond what is written in Scripture of the end times, we go beyond His will—out into our own territory of invention," he states. If God has a timetable for doomsday, Alnor claims that "no one will know the times the Father has set." Alnor even suggests that doomsayers could very well be the false prophets the Bible warns of.

Alnor believes doomsayers have a tendency to make the horrifying tales of the twentieth century fit into the pattern of Scripture. "Take, for example, the Antichrist," he says. Ever since people first read of the Antichrist in the Bible, they "have tried to put a name to the man who would so fully embody the spirit that opposes Christ." Alnor objects to this. He says people too often identify political and spiritual leaders as the Antichrist simply because they do not like them.

Opposing Literal Interpretations

Many other critics also oppose the doomsday prophecies of fundamentalist Christians. Rick Phillips, author of *The Emergence of the Divine*

This illustration depicts the belief that all men will be judged by God at the end of the world.

Child, is one who thinks the Bible cannot be interpreted literally. He does not think the Second Coming will be a physical event. Instead, he says, it will be a new state of awareness within individuals. He writes, "There are a lot of people waiting for an incarnation of God . . . to come rescue us, to take us to heaven, to confirm our faith that there is a salvation. Personally, I hope that the Messiah never comes! . . . The Messiah is within our own consciousness—the Christ is not a person but an awareness of divinity."

John White, author of *The Meeting of Science and Spirit*, agrees with Phillips. He points out that people who watch television evangelists often hear the message that "the Kingdom is coming; the End is near; these are the last days; Jesus is coming in glory." And he points out that Christians are not the only ones who foresee the coming of a savior. "To Jews, he is the Messiah. To Muslims, he is the Iman

Evangelist Oral Roberts is one of many Christian preachers who have gained fame through television. Critics believe that many such preachers have misinterpreted the Bible and its prophecies.

Mahdi. To Buddhists, he is the Maitreya Buddha. To Hindus, he is the avatar of the age." Yet other religions do not expect their savior to float down out of the sky and save the world. In fact, White says, "Christendom, by and large, has departed from the Bible." White believes fundamentalists have confused the true intent of the Bible by putting words and ideas into the mouths of the prophets that they "never said or meant and . . . would thoroughly repudiate today."

A Spiritual Transformation?

With the threat of nuclear war, environmental deterioration, and increasing reports of poverty, famine, crime, and natural disasters, it is understandable that people want someone to save them, White says. But he does not believe the Second Coming will occur as described in the Bible. Jesus will not appear physically. Like Phillips, White believes the Second Coming of Jesus will signal a state of divinity within individuals. The fundamentalists' need for a savior, he says, is "a childish wish, a fantasy based on immature awareness and poor biblical scholarship." Christ will appear at the deepest level of a person's being, not in the sky, White believes.

White and Phillips maintain that Christ is a spiritual consciousness that is the source of every individual's existence. The problem is that people have ignored this spiritual aspect of their being. If they can increase their awareness, they can evolve into higher levels of being. White and Phillips say meditation is one technique people can use to attain the necessary state of awareness. "The final appearance of Christ will not be a man in the sky," says White, but "an evolutionary event" marking the disappearance of selfishness in people. Even today, White and Phillips see this happening to more people. Eventually, everyone could be living on the same level of divine being that Jesus did, they say.

A charitable group in Washington, D.C., provides Thanksgiving dinner for the homeless. Some people believe that unselfish actions like these are also a sign of the end of the world—the world of selfishness and egotism, conquered by the human spirit.

Peter Roche de Coppens, author of *Apocalypse Now*, also believes biblical descriptions of Armageddon are not to be taken literally. Rather than a physical war, Armageddon will be a battle within people, de Coppens believes. He says that everyone has a lower and a higher self. The lower self is the ego and personality. Its goal is to take, to increase possessions and power in the world. It serves itself and no one else. The higher self is a person's eternal spirit. Its goal is to give, to share, to enhance and support life rather than destroy it. It strives for the good of the whole society, not just for the ego. De Coppens views Armageddon as a battle between these two selves. It is a spiritual transformation that takes place many times. He believes there will not be a worldwide Armageddon. Instead, each individual must fight his or her own battle.

Writing in the foreword to de Coppens's book, Father John Rossner criticizes fundamentalist views of Armageddon and the Antichrist. They are dangerous ideas, he says, that could lead to a destructive war before the time for the Second Coming is actually here. Citing Grace Halsell's book *Prophecy and Politics*, he writes:

> One may discover what depressing things can happen in the real world when Christian Fundamentalists . . . and politicians team up to use the Bible . . . "as an almanac for predictions of a [final] war.". . . By projecting one's personal and/or supposed national "enemies" into the "Anti-Christ" to be destroyed, and by convincing oneself and one's flock that Armageddon refers to an inevitable . . . contest between Russia and the United States [for example] to yield the holocaust required "before Christ can come again."

Rossner's concern is that fundamentalists could create a self-fulfilling prophecy of destruction because of their beliefs.

Fundamentalist Hal Lindsey disagrees with critics like Alnor, Phillips, White, de Coppens, and Rossner. He points out that more than three hundred prophecies in the Old Testament predicted Christ's initial appearance on earth. More than five hundred references speak of the Second Coming. Since the first prophecies were true, Lindsey believes, the ones regarding the Second Coming will be, also.

"Keep your eyes on the Middle East. If this is the time that we believe it is, this area will become a constant source of tension for all the world. . . . It will become so severe that only Christ or the Antichrist can solve it."

Hal Lindsey, *The Late Great Planet Earth*

"Often the catastrophist is driven by the desire to prove that the Bible or parts of it are literally true, though he may not easily acknowledge or even understand the emotional basis of his beliefs."

Daniel Cohen, *Waiting for the Apocalypse*

Three

Will Doomsday Come from the Sky?

Nostradamus, the great sixteenth-century astronomer and prophet, made this prediction about the end of the world:

A great spherical mountain of seven stades
[about a mile in diameter]
At a time when peace will give way to war,
Famine and flooding
It will roll end over end, sinking great nations.

Interpreters of his often ambiguous prophecies suggest that Nostradamus envisioned a mighty comet or other space object colliding with and destroying the earth. Present-day psychic Jeane Dixon has also predicted such an event. In the mid-1950s, she said, "Earthquakes and tidal waves will befall us as a result of the tremendous impact [of a celestial object] . . . in one of our oceans." Could such a catastrophe really occur? Some people believe it is inevitable.

Understanding Earth's Evolvement

Most scientists view the development of the earth in one of two ways. One theory is uniformitarianism. This is the idea that the earth's physical changes occur in orderly, small steps. Uniformitarians believe that the laws of nature that regulated the initial formation of the earth are still in operation,

(Opposite page) The appearance of a celestial death's-head in this seventeenth-century woodcut symbolizes the artist's belief that a passing comet is an omen of death and destruction. Will a comet bring the end of the world?

Moraſt.

governing all changes. Science writers Vernon Blackmore and Andrew Page, in *Evolution: The Great Debate*, describe the process: "Winds wear away mountains, glaciers transport huge boulders, volcanoes erupt and wreak . . . change." For uniformitarians, such natural and time-consuming forces explain how the geological features of the earth developed. Periodic ice ages, the rise and fall of sea levels, and periods of mountain building and erosion are the result of natural processes.

In recent years, another view of earth changes has gained prominence. This view is called catastrophism. Catastrophists do not believe natural forces fully explain the earth's geological features. They believe sudden, dramatic, and often devastating events—called catastrophes—have caused many

In the 1970s, scientists predicted that this Alaskan glacier would soon begin to retreat as part of an orderly, natural process of the earth's evolution. Some scientists today, however, believe that the earth's evolutionary process is more catastrophic than orderly.

of the earth's changes. In *Cosmic Catastrophes*, scientists Clark R. Chapman and David Morrison write, "Long banished to the fringes of science, catastrophism is becoming respectable." It is beginning to replace the idea that the laws of nature are consistent over time. Many catastrophists believe that in the earth's long history, many "doomsdays" have occurred—events so catastrophic as to cause a complete alteration of the earth's physical nature and even to wipe out nearly all living things. These catastrophists believe such a thing could happen again.

Chapman and Morrison describe recent evidence that supports their view: "Pictures sent back by far-flung spacecraft revealed solar-system-wide evidence of catastrophic bombardments and worlds in upheaval. . . . More and more, [scientists] are willing to entertain the notion catastrophes may have had (or will have in the future) a dominant influence [on earth]."

Craters in Space

Catastrophism has changed the way scientists look at some previously gained information. For example, in 1610, astronomer Galileo Galilei observed the moon through his first telescope. He noted that it was covered with craters—shallow, roughly circular depressions. More recently, astronomers have estimated that the moon has at least thirty thousand craters. Where did they come from?

As recently as a generation ago, say Chapman and Morrison, "many geologists and astronomers thought the craters of the Moon were of volcanic origin." But today, most scientists believe they are the result of celestial impacts—space objects crashing into the surface. The reason for this change is the amount of evidence scientists have gathered about both volcanic and impact craters. They have discovered, for example, that the shapes, relative sizes, and mineral makeup of volcanic and impact

"Very often the catastrophist relies on mistranslations, or simply misinterprets the evidence to suit his own beliefs."

Daniel Cohen, *Waiting for the Apocalypse*

"Many knowledgeable, open-minded scientists are still wary of catastrophism of any sort."

Clark R. Chapman and David Morrison, *Cosmic Catastrophes*

Earth's moon is pock-marked with craters, some very large, resulting from the impact of meteors and other space debris.

craters tend to be very different from one another. Careful analysis of photographs of the moon's craters and of moon rocks brought back by astronauts has convinced many scientists that the moon's craters were largely caused by impacts.

Spacecraft have radioed back evidence of impacts on other planets as well. "A few moons and planets seem to have experienced impacts of such incredible violence that they were disrupted or dispersed," say Chapman and Morrison. A few moons and planets "were nearly broken apart and fell back together in a jumbled mass of fragments." Chapman and Morrison point out that the moon and the earth are subject to the "same rain of interplanetary debris." It is therefore quite possible that the earth will one day be hit by a large comet or other object, causing large-scale destruction.

In fact, the earth already has some of these craters. Meteor Crater in Arizona is similar to craters on the moon, Mars, and Mercury. It is four thousand feet in diameter and six hundred feet deep. The crater is evidence that something struck the earth about fifty thousand years ago. Scientists have determined that whatever hit was a small object, about two hundred feet in diameter. It was made of a nickel-iron alloy and weighed several million tons. Scientists believe the object was pulled into a collision course with the earth by the gravitational forces of other planets.

Another impact formed Ries Crater in Bavaria, Germany. This crater is fifteen million years old. Originally, the crater was three miles deep. Scientists estimate that the projectile that hit was one mile wide. The impact would have destroyed all life for hundreds of miles around and would have caused earthquakes around the world. This event doomed many of the creatures that existed at that time.

More than one hundred ancient craters with diameters as great as fifty miles have been docu-

Almost a mile across, Meteor Crater in Arizona is believed to have been made by a meteorite about two hundred feet in diameter, weighing several million tons.

mented around the planet. Other extraterrestrial objects may have hit in the oceans and cannot be found. Most of the craters gradually disappear because of erosion.

Celestial Objects

Our solar system contains billions of traveling objects smaller than the planets, moons, and sun. These include asteroids, comets, and meteors. Asteroids are small bodies ranging from a few miles to about five hundred miles in diameter. Most are found in a belt orbiting the sun in the space between Jupiter and Mars. They are often called minor planets because they are solid matter like the planets. Comets are generally smaller bodies that orbit the sun. They also range greatly in size, but they are not solid. They have a nucleus made up mainly of frozen gases that expands and contracts depending

Earth's solar system contains the sun, planets, moons, asteroids, comets, and innumerable meteors hurtling randomly among them. Dozens of meteors disintegrate daily in earth's atmosphere.

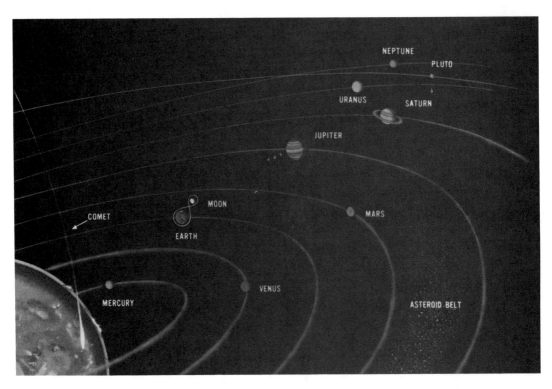

on how close it is to the sun. A brilliant corona surrounds the nucleus, and a tail made of gases and dust stretches out for millions of miles behind. A meteor is a small particle of interplanetary debris, such as a piece of an asteroid. Meteors become visible when they burst into flame upon entering the earth's oxygen-rich atmosphere. This is why they are commonly called shooting stars. A meteor that is not completely burned up after passing through the atmosphere is called a meteorite.

Was There a Planet?

Because the gap of space between Mars and Jupiter (where the asteroid belt orbits) is unusually large, some scientists believe a planet may have once existed there. In the 1970s, for example, Canadian physicist Michael Ovenden theorized that a Saturn-size planet existed there sixteen million years ago. He believes the present asteroid belt could be the remains of such a cosmic body. If Ovenden is right, the explosion must have been stupendous to have completely atomized the planet.

Chapman and Morrison are not so sure such a planet ever existed. They argue that the evidence against it is overwhelming:

> Not even Michael Ovenden himself could imagine a possible way for such a planet to explode. We *know* why stars explode [they are composed of explosive gases], but stellar forces cannot operate within planets. The asteroids themselves are in approximately circular orbits, not the chaotic . . . orbits one would expect for explosion debris. . . . The dispersal of a Saturn-mass of material . . . only 16 million years ago would have had a big effect on lunar soils . . . but there is no sign of such an event.

Science writer Daniel Cohen, however, suggests in his book *Waiting for the Apocalypse* that Ovenden could be right. The planet could have collided with another object, for example. Or perhaps "the

"The possibility of a comet's striking the earth . . . is considered extremely small, but not impossible."

Fred Warshofsky, *Doomsday: The Science of Catastrophe*

"There must have been many impacts of comets (and asteroids) with the Earth."

Carl Sagan and Ann Druyan, *Comet*

planet was blown apart during a thermonuclear war among its inhabitants," although Cohen admits that "this theory belongs more in the realm of science fiction." Nonetheless, if one planet has blown up, he says, "it could happen again."

To Cohen, the asteroid belt is not just a warning that a planet can blow up. The asteroids themselves are dangerous. Although they orbit in a path between Mars and Jupiter, they frequently bump into one another, occasionally causing one to be knocked out of orbit. Also, they can sometimes be thrown out of orbit by the gravitational pull of other celestial bodies. Sometimes, these wild asteroids sail near the earth. In 1932, one came within 2 million miles; in 1936, 1 million miles; in 1937, 485,000 miles; and in 1989, one came within 500,000 miles. These last two were very close. Five hundred thousand miles is only twice the distance to the moon. Dick Teresi and Judith Hooper say that if an asteroid this size ever hit the earth at its flying speed of forty-six thousand miles per hour, the impact "would have obliterated New York City or Los Angeles. It would have carved out a crater half a mile deep and five miles wide. A water impact . . . would have created waves several hundred meters high that could have swept over coastal areas."

Dangerous Asteroids

Cohen cites astronomer Robert S. Richardson who wrote in 1965 of the possibility of an asteroid hitting the earth someday. Richardson said, "We are aware of these close-approaching asteroids only through the accident of discovery. No one knows how many . . . may pass near the earth each year without being noticed."

Unlike bright comets, asteroids are hidden in the darkness of space. They are hard to detect. Furthermore, Cohen says that Dr. Harold Mazursky of the U.S. Geological Survey "believes that large im-

pacts are more frequent than is commonly believed by his colleagues." Of special concern are large asteroids called Apollos. These asteroids are known to cross the earth's orbit. Astronomer Eugene Shoemaker believes there could be up to eleven hundred asteroids larger than 1 kilometer (0.6 mile). Cohen asks, "Are there [objects] out in space that are large enough to cause a worldwide cataclysm if they struck the earth? And if so, do such objects regularly enter the vicinity of the earth?" The answer is yes. In the asteroid belt, asteroids range from 485 miles in diameter to the size of basketballs. Cohen explains that "the material is sparsely spread through space. A spaceship passing through the belt would encounter an asteroid only by chance. But

In this painting, an asteroid five hundred miles in diameter strikes the earth.

there is enough material out there for astronomers to realize that something happened or failed to happen in that segment of the solar system."

Historians have recorded many instances of apparent asteroid activity, frequently in June. For example, in June 783, fireballs streaking over the earth terrified the witnesses. On June 25, 1178, the moon was struck by an object whose energy was ten times greater than all the nuclear arsenals on earth. In June 1975, a swarm of boulders struck the moon at a speed of sixty-seven thousand miles per hour.

Science writers Victor Clube and Bill Napier, in their book *The Cosmic Winter*, ask, "Why late June? What is the nature of these events? And what is the actual threat they pose to [humanity]?. . . It has been found that there is a great swarm of cosmic debris circulating in a potentially dangerous orbit." The debris cuts across the earth's orbit in June and November every few thousand years. Could asteroids bombard the earth again someday, causing widespread destruction? According to Clube and Napier, "An unrecognized hazard is out there; . . . at

The comet Kohoutek flashed by earth in 1974. But the earth has not always been so lucky. Scientists believe a comet devastated a remote region of Siberia in 1908.

[such] a strike, civilization could be plunged into a new Dark Age."

Harold Mazursky suggests that asteroids should be tracked so that if they come near the earth, they can be blasted by nuclear missiles. Otherwise, asks Daniel Cohen, "What would happen if something really big, a hundred miles across or more, struck the earth?. . . It would dig a crater about the size of the Pacific Ocean." According to Cohen, one theory is that a massive collision did form the Pacific Ocean basin at some time in the past. Such an impact would set off volcanoes and shift the earth's crust. In addition, the impact could blow the planet's atmosphere into space. "Not only would every living thing in the impact zone be killed, but every living thing on earth would die," says Cohen. "Even if [people] could somehow survive the shock waves, the earthquakes, tidal waves, and volcanic action," they would die without an atmosphere. Cohen concludes, "That truly would spell the end of the world."

Closer Encounters: Comets

On June 30, 1908, an object exploded over Tunguska, a remote area in northern Siberia. Its energy was equivalent to that of a large hydrogen bomb. It lit up the sky like a fire, and people witnessed the glow throughout Russia, Europe, and western Siberia.

The Tunguska area is in one of the most inaccessible spots on earth. That and the tumultuous political events of the time prevented a research team from reaching the site until 1927. The object, probably a comet, disintegrated five miles above the earth. Its explosion flattened the surrounding forest for a distance of forty miles. Eighty million trees were felled. Scientist and author Carl Sagan says that "an atmospheric shock wave . . . twice circled the earth." Could it happen again? According to astronomer Leonard Kulik, "There is no reason what-

A small part of the northern Siberian forest devastated by the 1908 explosion of a comet or other extraterrestrial body five miles above the planet's surface.

ever why a similar visitation should not fall at any moment upon a more populous region."

For more than one million years, people have watched thousands of comets come and go. Often, they have been regarded as omens of change or ill fortune. Carl Sagan and Ann Druyan, authors of *Comet*, report that comets had different meanings to different people: "To the Masai of East Africa, a comet meant famine; to the Zulu of South Africa, war; to the Djaga of Zaire, specifically smallpox."

The ancient Chinese collected a large body of data on comets throughout history. Li Ch'an Feng (602-667) wrote in *Records of World's Change*, "Comets are vile stars. Every time they appear in the south, something happens to wipe out the old and establish the new. . . . In Sung, Ch'i, and later Ch'in times, when a comet appeared in the Constellation of the Big Dipper, all soldiers died in chaos. . . . When a comet travels north but points south the country has a major calamity. . . . There are floods."

A famous comet is Halley's comet. It last appeared in 1986. It can be seen every seventy-six years as it orbits the sun. In 1910, many people feared Halley's comet would collide with the earth, bringing doomsday. But astronomers knew that its head was not within millions of miles of the earth. The earth was going to pass harmlessly through the tail.

In general, comets can be frightening spectacles. They appear as huge fireballs in the sky, a terrifying sight to someone gazing up from below.

According to scientists, the amount of damage caused by a small comet, like an asteroid, would depend on where it hit. An impact in a city could kill millions of people, many more than died in the atomic bomb blast over Hiroshima in World War II.

The incredible devastation caused to Hiroshima by an atomic bomb blast in 1945 is small compared to what would happen if a comet or asteroid slammed into a major city.

A drawing depicts the Oort cloud of comets that scientists believe surrounds our solar system (center). Scientists estimate the cloud contains 100 billion comets.

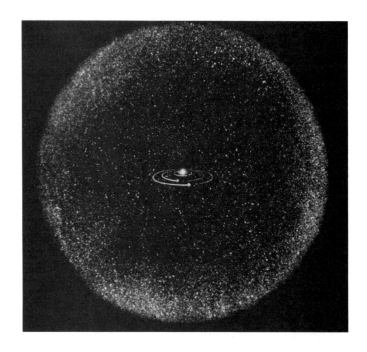

Comets generally originate in the Oort cloud, a sphere of 100 billion comets that scientists believe surrounds our solar system. Occasionally, comets are deflected toward the inner solar system, passing by the earth. Others get trapped by gravitational fields of the outer planets and simply orbit around them. According to Chapman and Morrison, a comet that crosses the orbit of a big planet "is a danger to the planet" because eventually the two objects may meet. Chapman and Morrison believe that objects as large as ten kilometers (six miles) in diameter must run into our planet every fifty or one hundred years or so.

What damage could a comet ten kilometers in size and weighing one trillion tons do? It would carve out a crater more than one hundred miles wide. It would penetrate the earth's mantle, the layer between the earth's core and crust. The impact would loft 100 trillion tons of pulverized rock into the atmosphere. If the impact occurred in the ocean, huge tidal waves would spread over the planet. According to Chapman and Morrison, such an impact is inevitable. Someday, it will happen.

Mass Extinctions Caused by Comets?

Some scientists believe comets may have already caused such massive catastrophes. According to Chapman and Morrison, "Our cosmic neighborhood is a vast shooting gallery of comets and asteroids in which the Earth itself could hardly have remained unscathed."

Chapman and Morrison point to evidence that more than a dozen mass extinctions—more than a dozen doomsdays—have occurred in the past 570 million years. A huge one occurred 65 million years ago when the dinosaurs disappeared. Another great extinction happened 250 million years ago. Scientists estimate that three-quarters of all existing species died at that time. More than 95 percent of individual ocean species were killed.

Other major extinctions took place 215, 360, and 435 million years ago. For every species alive today, hundreds of others have become extinct. Minor extinctions have also happened. Two occurred 12 and 38 million years ago. The last four known extinctions happened at intervals of 25 to 30 million years. Are these extinctions random or regular occurrences? According to Chapman and Morrison, they seem to be regular. Other scientists agree.

Geologists David Raup and Jack Sepkoski of the University of Chicago claim that regular extinctions take place every twenty-six million years or so. They determined this by studying fossil-bearing rock and sediment layers in the ocean. They found that layers of fossils occurred at twenty-six-million-year intervals.

Other scientists have tried to confirm this theory, which is called periodicity because it proposes that extinctions happen at regular periods. In April 1984, geologists at the University of California at

"The sudden destruction or emergence of land areas by earthquakes or volcanoes is limited in extent. Past examples have seldom caused a loss of more than fifty or sixty square miles of territory at a time."

William H. Stiebing Jr., *Ancient Astronauts, Cosmic Collisions*

"Scientists now recognize that the universe is dynamic and tumultuous—a place of change, often violent and catastrophic."

Clark R. Chapman and David Morrison, *Cosmic Catastrophes*

University of Chicago geologists Jack Sepkoski (left) and David Raup theorize that mass extinctions due to comets crashing into the earth occur at regular, twenty-six-million-year intervals.

Astronomer Carl Sagan concludes from the theory of periodicity that somewhere in space there is a comet with earth's name on it just waiting to bring doomsday.

Berkeley found evidence of a twenty-eight-million-year periodicity for impact craters on earth. Two NASA (National Aeronautics and Space Administration) scientists discovered evidence of thirty-one-million-year periodicities. These different conclusions about periodicity may not be significant because scientists cannot precisely measure the age of ancient craters and rocks.

Although the evidence in support of the theory of periodicity appears good, some scientists have raised objections. According to Chapman and Morrison, only a small number—approximately twenty—of these ancient craters have been dated, and the date calculations may not be reliable enough to support the theory.

Astronomer and author Carl Sagan thinks mass extinctions might occur regularly as the result of bombardments from comets: "If there are periodicities, a stunning connection between life down here on Earth and events up there in the sky has been uncovered. In that case, somewhere a cosmic doomsday clock is ticking away even now." If the last extinction occurred twelve million years ago, then the next may not occur for fourteen million years, given the past pattern.

The Evidence

Evidence of cometary impacts was found by the late Luis Alvarez, a physicist at the University of California at Berkeley, and his son Walter Alvarez, a geologist. In the late 1970s, they became interested in a geological layer of sediment that signals the transition between the Cretaceous and Tertiary periods in earth history. The transition marks a major turning point for the evolution of life on the

University of California at Berkeley scientists Luis and Walter Alvarez identify a layer of sediment they believe proves a meteor hit the earth millions of years ago, wiping out the dinosaurs.

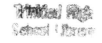

A painting depicts pterodactyls soaring above the earth about sixty-five million years ago, as a great meteor strikes the planet. Such a catastrophe may have caused the dinosaurs' demise.

planet: the dinosaurs of the Cretaceous period were replaced by mammals as the dominant life-form.

At the point where the periods meet in the earth layer, "There is a sudden change in the fossil population of small marine organisms," Chapman and Morrison explain. Some of these organisms were called forams. In the lower, older rock are countless shells of different forams. Just above the layer, or boundary, most of the shells do not exist. This indicates a mass extinction.

At the boundary layer, the Alvarezes discovered a thin layer of clay that is found all over the world. The layer contains a rare metal called iridium. The concentration of iridium is thirty times higher in the boundary layer than above or below it. Where did such a large amount come from? The Alvarezes knew that most of the iridium on earth originated in extraterrestrial objects. Since most dinosaur fossils occur below the clay layer but not above it, the scientists concluded that the extinction and the iridium are related. Carl Sagan remarks, "A worldwide iridium-rich layer marking the end of the Cretaceous looks very much like direct evidence that a large cosmic body struck the earth 65 million years ago." The Alvarezes were convinced that this was true. They determined that the object probably weighed one trillion tons and was six miles in diameter, not an unusual size for either a comet or an asteroid.

The explosion of the impact would have been huge. More important than the impact is that 100 trillion tons of dust would have been lofted into the atmosphere. Chapman and Morrison claim:

> Scientists have calculated that this quantity of dust would have produced a pall over the whole globe with a duration of at least several months. During this period of global darkness, neither light nor heat [would have been] available to sustain life. With photosynthesis [the ability of plants to turn sunlight into food] and the Earth plunged into deep cold, it is no wonder there was a great dying.

Other Explanations

Yet some critics are not convinced that the impact theory is true. Chapman and Morrison comment, "One of the most serious . . . objections [to the Alvarezes' theory] is the absence of any 100-mile-diameter crater in the Earth with an age of 65 million years. Without a corpse, it is difficult to establish that a murder took place." But while no such crater has been found on land, there is the possibility that one exists on the ocean floor. In fact, a search is underway. Planetary scientists Alan Hildebrand and William Boynton of the University of Arizona have been looking for a crater in the ocean. According to a 1990 article in *Discover* magazine, they have found on geologic maps of the Caribbean what appears to be a circular depression that might be a crater. They hope that by studying the site with sonar and by taking core samples, they will be able to determine the truth.

Even if Hildebrand and Boynton are unsuccessful, other explanations for the dinosaur extinction are possible. Chapman and Morrison write, "Many geologists are familiar with volcanic eruptions, and it is natural to ask if a giant volcanic explosion might also produce a global cloud of dust." However, volcano eruptions would not produce the iridium enhancement in other minerals in the clay layer. This can be created only by an impact. Worldwide, the boundary layer contains shocked quartz.

Victor Clube and Bill Napier, in their book *The*

Washington's Mount St. Helens blows its top. The 1980 eruption spewed tons of ash twelve miles into the sky. Some scientists believe that millions of years ago, much of the life on earth was destroyed when a cloud of ash covered the planet after an enormous volcanic eruption.

A geologist photographs a geyser of lava shooting up from Hawaii's Mauna Kilauea. Lava has been found to be rich in the metal iridium, which is also found in meteorites. Some scientists take this as evidence that perhaps volcanoes, not meteors, wiped out the dinosaurs.

Cosmic Winter, disagree that the impact theory explains all. They think volcanoes could, in fact, be the cause of the extinctions. For example, they point out that the January 1983 eruption of Kilauea in Hawaii left "very large concentrations of arsenic, selenium and other elements found in high abundance at the . . . boundary. The particles were also found to be strikingly rich in iridium." Despite this information, most scientists favor the impact theory.

A Death Star?

Some astronomers believe the sun may have a small companion star, and Carl Sagan and Ann Druyan suggest that the star's orbit may bring it close to the Oort cloud. "With such an orbit," they write in *Comet*, "once every 30 million years the companion would plow through the denser parts of the Oort cloud, and shower the Earth . . . with comets." Scientists named this undiscovered star Nemesis, or death star, "after the Greek goddess who visited just punishment on the self-righteous," according to Sagan and Druyan. Since no one has proof that Nemesis exists, all that can be said is that it *might* have brushed the Oort cloud twelve million years ago when the last impact occurred.

Sagan and Druyan write, "There is at least one major search . . . designed specifically to catch a companion star, if one exists. If it *is* found, few will doubt that it is the principal cause of periodic mass extinctions." Otherwise, the authors believe, the theory "will remain provocative but unproved."

If it does exist, Nemesis should now be on the far side of the sun. Scientists think it is two light-years (about twelve trillion miles) from the sun, or halfway to the nearest known star, Alpha Centauri.

A Companion to the Sun

Victor Clube and Bill Napier point out that companion stars, also called binary stars, are common. Binary stars revolve around one another, and the gravitational pull of each keeps the other in orbit. But if Nemesis is out there, it and the sun are too far apart to be normal binary stars. The gravitational forces would be too weak to keep Nemesis in orbit. It should have been tossed into deep space. Clube and Napier suggest that scientists who support this idea have not done their homework. They write, "It seems quite extraordinary that a [theory] so lacking in scientific depth has spawned so much attention even within the scientific community."

Chapman and Morrison suggest another explanation for the Oort cloud disruptions. Scientists know that the sun bobs up and down as it moves through space. To move from an up position to a down position takes thirty to thirty-five million years. This is close to the twenty-five to thirty million years theorists have established for the impact intervals. The sun's bobbing might disturb space debris that gets pulled into the inner solar system, sending it toward earth. The problem with this explanation is that the sun just reached the halfway point in its bobbing in the last two million years. It was at that time that it last stirred up space debris. But the last extinction occurred twelve million years ago.

Planet X

Some say the mysterious culprit that causes impacts might be a planet. Science writer Frank Close, in his book *Apocalypse When?,* discusses the possibility that a tenth planet exists beyond Pluto. Pluto is the planet farthest from the sun. "We don't know where or how far away it [the tenth planet] is with any confidence, but we suspect it is larger than the Earth," Close says. He thinks it probably takes this unknown planet a thousand years to orbit the sun.

There is some evidence to support the theory that another planet exists. Scientists know that if a planet shows an odd motion, it happens because a neighboring planet tugs it with a gravitational pull. Neptune was discovered in the nineteenth century and Pluto in the twentieth, only after scientists noticed unusual motions in other planets, especially Uranus. After figuring out mathematically that the planets must exist and then diligently studying the predicted orbits with sophisticated equipment, scientists found the two new planets. They were surprised to discover that Neptune had an unusual motion as well. Since Pluto is too small to affect Neptune, scientists theorized that there could be still another planet beyond Pluto.

In recent decades, however, the orbits of Uranus and Neptune have been normal. Close explains, "This suggests that Planet X was near the planets 100 years ago but is now far out" in space. If it does exist, is Planet X responsible for the regular extinctions? According to Close, "Planet X may well exist, but it is unlikely to be responsible. . . . The inner edge of the Oort cloud is at least 20 times more remote and beyond the influence of Planet X in a normal orbit." Consequently, say Chapman and Morrison, "We are left with a great mystery. There is evidence . . . that much of the history of our planet and of the evolution of life" depends on a source in space that causes impacts approximately every thirty million years. But scientists have not yet agreed on what that source is.

Will the Earth Be Struck Again?

According to Daniel Cohen, it is not very likely that a comet will collide with the earth. Space is so vast that the chance of the earth and a comet being in the same place at the same time is slight, he

The black dots on this map show the locations of suspected impact craters.

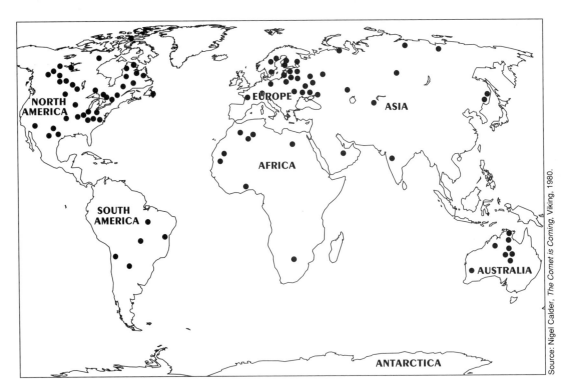

Source: Nigel Calder, *The Comet is Coming*, Viking, 1980.

claims. Yet the earth could be devastated by something else. Cohen does admit that a great extinction, like that of the dinosaurs, could happen again. "The next time the victims may be [people]," he says.

Frank Close disagrees with Cohen's assessment. "There's less than a 1 in a billion chance that we and a comet" will collide, he says. "But if there are 100 billion comets in the Oort cloud, and if as few as 1 in 100 is disturbed by a passing star, then 1 billion comets have entered the solar system. This makes it almost certain that a comet will hit us some day." Also, Close claims that scientists estimate that there are as many as eight undetected comets for every one that *is* detected. Close suggests that a comet hits the earth every ten million years or so. "Once in 100 million years we may hit a real monster," he states.

Four

Will Natural Disasters End the World?

Japan and Europe fall into the sea. China is covered with snow and ice. New land appears in the South Pacific. Giant earthquakes destroy much of California and the East Coast of the United States. They also hit Italy, Greece, Russia, Turkey, China, and the Himalaya Mountains. Volcanoes erupt in Africa. If some doomsayers are right, the world may be destroyed not by a missile from space but by natural disasters such as these. The earth itself might destroy civilization.

The Sleeping Prophet

American prophet Edgar Cayce identified this concept as destruction by earth changes. Cayce was called the Sleeping Prophet because he received most of his prophetic information from a supernatural source while he was in a sleeplike trance. In the 1930s, Cayce forecast that many physical upheavals would occur on the earth throughout the last decades of the twentieth century. The biggest and the worst upheavals would happen in the final ten years. These would include devastating earthquakes, volcano eruptions, flooding, dramatic sinking and rising of land, and coastlines falling away. In the year 2000 or 2001, a pole shift will occur,

(Opposite page) A family staggers from their ruined house after their small Greek island, Santorini, was rocked by a 1956 earthquake and tidal wave. Will earthquakes someday destroy the world?

Edgar Cayce, America's "sleeping prophet," predicted that cataclysmic changes would occur on earth in the last decades of the twentieth century.

Cayce predicted. The earth will tumble end over end for several days. As a result, new climates and geographies will be established.

Earth Changes

Cayce specified what will happen and where. In the United States, he said:

> All over the country many physical changes of a minor or greater degree [will occur]. . . . Many portions of the East Coast will be disturbed, as well as . . . the West Coast, as well as the central portion of the United States. Los Angeles, San Francisco, most all of these will be among those [cities] that will be destroyed before New York, even. The waters of the Great Lakes will empty into the Gulf of Mexico.

Earth changes will strike the rest of the world, too, Cayce believed. In Europe, he claimed, "the upper portion . . . will be changed as in the twinkling of an eye." In Japan, "the greater portion . . . must go into the sea." Of the world in general, Cayce said, "The earth will be broken up in many places. The early portion will see a change in the physical aspect of the west coast of America. . . . There will be new lands seen off the Caribbean Sea, and dry land will appear. . . . South America shall be shaken up from the uppermost portion to the end."

J. R. Jochmans predicts in his book *Rolling Thunder* that the 1990s will host huge earthquakes. He writes that the Richter scale, "which measures degrees of earthquake intensity from 1 to 10 (each number representing ten times the destructive power of the previous number) will have to be revised to include *an 11 and a 12*." The California coastline, he says, will drop off into the sea, and the Pacific Ocean will reach to Nebraska.

The Bible's Book of Revelation also speaks of cataclysmic changes: "The earth will reel like a drunkard and it will sway like a hut . . . until it falls, never to rise again."

Medicine man Sun Bear of the Chippewa Bear tribe is another forecaster who predicts coming earth changes. In his book *Black Dawn, Bright Day*, he describes his dreams and visions of these future changes:

> Over a period of time I have had many, many dreams that showed the coming of the Earth changes. So have other people. . . . I saw a time when cities wouldn't exist in their present state. During the changes the most dangerous places will be near cities with nuclear and chemical plants. . . . In the next ten to fifteen years, you're going to see such major changes at all levels that you won't recognize the earth afterwards. Awareness of the Earth changes is growing. The truth about them is in the papers daily now. Weather changes, natural disasters, more earthquakes . . . all these are hard to ignore.

Sun Bear explains further why he believes these earth changes must occur:

Chippewa Indian medicine man and author Sun Bear believes that the earth is a living being. He affirms that great changes will occur on earth as part of the living earth's growth and development.

To Native people, the Earth is a living, intelligent being. It is capable of making the necessary changes for its own survival. These changes might not be convenient for humans, but the Earth will make them anyway. . . . We are the same as deer and other creatures that begin to die when they get too far out of balance, or out of harmony with the path they're supposed to be on.

According to Sun Bear, earth changes will result in the death of 75 to 90 percent of the world's population.

Earthquakes

Earthquakes are terrible and destructive for the people, animals, and environment that must endure them. *The Powers of Nature*, published by the National Geographic Society, describes the experiences of earthquake survivors, including Elena Enache of Bucharest, Romania:

> The shaking stopped in less than a minute. Retired schoolteacher Elena Enache lay in total darkness, conscious but stunned, gagging on plaster dust and wondering what had become of her normal, routine world. Only seconds earlier she had been knitting and watching television; then her high-rise apartment in Bucharest had shuddered violently, bouncing her up and down. Ceilings had given way; tons of debris had rained down—all just before the lights went out on March 4, 1977. . . . Suddenly she realized the truth: an earthquake had leveled her apartment building—and she was buried alive.

Enache was lucky. She lived. Many people do not survive major earthquakes. For example, on May 31, 1970, 68,000 people died from an earthquake in Chimbote, Peru. On June 28, 1976, a quake measuring 8.2 on the Richter scale killed 800,000 in China. In December 1988, a quake killed 60,000 in Armenia in the Soviet Union. In June 1990, a 7.7 quake killed 50,000 in Iran. According to Sun Bear, between 1950 and 1990, the number of quakes greater than 6.0 on the Richter scale nearly doubled compared to the first fifty years of the century. When a quake kills more than 1,000 people, it is called a killer earthquake. Since 1970, twenty-four of these have occurred. Sun Bear says they are becoming more intense.

Some scientists agree that the earth might be moving closer to having superquakes. Scientists routinely determine the energy of quakes and keep careful records of their levels of intensity. So far, no earthquake has exceeded about 8.6 or 8.7 on the Richter scale. But the records could be deceptive, say seismologists Michael Chinnery and Robert G. North of the Massachusetts Institute of Technology. They wrote in *Science* magazine that quakes four times as powerful as those recorded in recent years may arrive within the next fifty years. They say, "It

A ruptured and displaced roadway testifies to the earth's movement during the 1976 killer earthquake in China that extinguished 800,000 human lives.

is not clear that the record of large earthquakes during the last 100 years is sufficiently detailed that the occurrence of such a catastrophic event can be ruled out."

Many experts agree that even if quakes do not destroy the entire world, the "big one" will occur in California in the foreseeable future. Geologist T.A. Heppenheimer states in his book *The Coming Quake*:

> A catastrophe is haunting southern California. . . . Within the lifetimes of most of its people, Los Angeles and its communities stand to be ripped apart. . . . It will take place along the San Andreas Fault, a far-reaching gash in the bedrock of California that runs from the Mexican border well to the north of San Francisco. Along the southern portions of this fault, for a length of as much as two hundred miles, deep and extensive masses of rock will suddenly shift and move.

No part of the country is safe, however, from great earthquakes, according to Heppenheimer. Some scientists believe that the greatest danger is in the Midwest around the New Madrid fault in Missouri. A huge earthquake that hit there in 1811 and 1812 affected a wider area than the great San Francisco quake of 1906. Considerable danger also exists near Seattle and other areas in the Pacific Northwest.

What Causes Earthquakes?

Ancient civilizations believed that the earth rested atop a giant animal or god that occasionally moved, causing the earth to tremble. The Algonquian tribe in America believed the world rested on the back of a tortoise. Japanese myths say that the world rides on the back of a wriggling catfish. The Norse people blamed earthquakes on their quarreling gods.

Today, most scientists believe earthquakes are caused by the movement and collision of large pieces of the earth. Jonathan Weiner, in his book *Planet Earth*, explains how this movement happens, a concept called plate tectonics:

> The Earth's outer shell, some sixty miles thick, is cracked like a giant eggshell. It is fractured into many huge slabs (somewhere between a dozen and twenty), which because of their rigidity are called *plates*. The plates are not anchored to the planet, but drift about, rubbing and chafing and sometimes crashing against one another. . . . [This is] all in slow motion, and it is this that makes earthquakes.

Cracks along the earth, called faults, indicate where plates rub together below the earth's surface. As plates slide and grind, pressure builds up along

A ruined apartment building teeters in the background as stunned survivors of the 1988 Armenian earthquake dig for belongings amid the rubble.

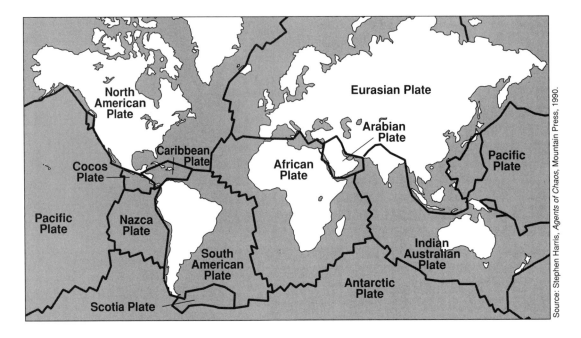

Source: Stephen Harris, *Agents of Chaos*, Mountain Press, 1990.

The gigantic, shifting plates that comprise the earth's crust are outlined on this world map. The plates continually push against each other. When they shift, an earthquake occurs.

the faults. When the tension gets too high, the plates slip and an earthquake happens.

Entire continents rest on top of the plates. The United States rests on what is called the North American plate. The plates can be thousands of miles wide and forty to eighty miles thick. Earthquakes occur most frequently where two continental plates meet or where a continental plate meets an oceanic plate. In California, the North American plate rubs against the Pacific plate, which is why California is a high-risk earthquake zone. The 1989 San Francisco quake relieved only some of the pressure that had built up since the last major quake in 1906. California is crisscrossed with major faults.

Other High-Risk Zones

Such zones exist elsewhere in the world as well. Japan, for instance, is a high-risk zone. In the town of Matsushiro, 120 miles northwest of Tokyo, a series of quakes that began in August 1965 lasted until 1977. According to Dr. Mamoru Katsumata, chief researcher at the Matsushiro Seismological Observatory, there were 722,665 quakes during that period. As many as 10,000 quakes occurred in a single day, although most of them were small and unnoticeable. From Tokyo to 180 miles south of the city, major quakes have hit Japan's east coast once every eighty-five years. Oddly enough, the region southwest of Tokyo has not had a major quake since 1854.

Will parts of Japan sink because of earthquakes? Just as in California, a big earthquake is expected and could be as devastating as a nuclear war.

Japan, like California, lies along an earthquake fault that belongs to a belt extending from Alaska, down California, to South America. Other high-risk

Viewed from the air, California's San Andreas Fault, the crack between the Pacific plate and the North American plate, is clearly visible.

areas exist in the Mediterranean coastal areas of Italy and Greece and in the Himalaya Mountains in Asia.

Disagreeing with Doomsayers

Will California actually sink into the ocean? No, according to Jonathan Weiner. He writes:

> Despite popular misconceptions, California will not sink into the Pacific. It will instead slide ever northward. In 15 million years, Los Angeles, if it still exists, will be a suburb of San Francisco. The Giants and Dodgers will again be crosstown rivals. . . . As the Pacific Plate slides by, a piece of the west coast rides with it and it is being carried off to the north.

Eventually, California will end up near the Aleutian Islands in Alaska, he believes.

Others agree that California is not in great danger of destruction, despite the increase in earthquakes. Dr. Charles Richter, inventor of the Richter scale, lived in California. He believed the risk is highly exaggerated. He said:

> One notices with some amusement that certain religious groups have picked this rather unfortunate time to insist that the number of earthquakes is increasing. In part they are misled by the increasing number of small earthquakes that are being catalogued and listed by newer, more sensitive [seismological] stations throughout the world.

More quakes occurred from 1896 to 1906 than occur today, he said, and none has ever been above 9.0 on the scale.

Popular science fiction author Isaac Asimov also disagreed with doomsayers about earthquakes. Certainly, Asimov claimed, an earthquake will happen along the San Andreas Fault. But movement along that fault will be only a few meters at the most. He stated that earthquakes have never been destroyers of entire civilizations.

"And there shall be earthquakes in diverse places."

The Bible, Matthew 24:7

"No known geological forces can account for the sudden destruction of a continent."

William H. Stiebing Jr., *Ancient Astronauts, Cosmic Collisions*

Charles Richter invented the Richter scale which measures the intensity of earthquakes. Fully aware of California's high earthquake activity, Richter nonetheless believed the state was safe enough to make his home there.

John White, author of *The Meeting of Science and Spirit*, agrees. He writes that in all of recorded history, "there has been nothing even remotely resembling the loss of the West Coast, with the Pacific Ocean flowing inland through many states."

Continental Drift

The idea that continents are mere passengers on the backs of the plates that make up the earth's crust was first proposed in 1910. German explorer Alfred Wegener noticed the jigsawlike fit between the western coast of Africa and the eastern coast of South America. Wegener did not believe the fit was

German explorer-scientist Alfred Wegener theorized in 1910 that the earth's continents had once been a single great landmass that gradually split apart.

coincidence. He believed the two continents might have been one in the past and had split apart.

What was his evidence? A mountain range in South Africa runs from east to west. Another range matches it on the other side of the Atlantic. According to Jonathan Weiner, "A plateau in Brazil corresponds neatly to another in Africa's Ivory Coast. Possibly a primitive fern, *Glossopteris*, [is] common in certain parts of both Africa and Brazil." He adds that the plateaus "line up as neatly as their coastlines." Wegener believed that fitting the coastlines together would be just like refitting the torn pieces of a newspaper by matching their edges. Then, one could check to see that the lines of print ran smoothly across.

Wegener's work has led many scientists to conclude that there was once a single supercontinent. Scientists call it Pangaea, which is Greek for "all land." They believe it broke into several pieces and that the continents are still drifting apart. Measurements show that North America and Europe draw farther apart each year—by about two inches. If they are drifting now, it is possible they have been doing so for millions of years.

No Speedy Changes

Could continental drift end the world? Yes, according to scientists, but it will take about fifty million years. Then, they think, the shifting landmasses will displace water from one area to another, raising sea levels and flooding Central America. The Atlantic and the Pacific oceans will merge in the Caribbean. The eastern and western shores of the Americas will be underwater. Fifty million years is an estimate, but scientists know the continents and the earth will continue to change drastically. Jonathan Weiner comments, "It is hard to imagine that the continents are adrift, ferried about on great fragments of the earth's shell. . . . What we have been pleased to call 'Solid Earth' is not as solid as

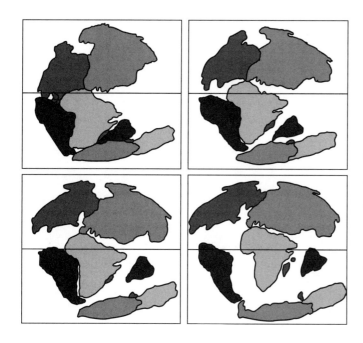

An artist's rendition of continental drift. From a single landmass called Pangaea (upper left), the continents drifted toward their present-day positions.

we thought. It is energetic, dynamic, and . . . restless." Continents could indeed split apart, destroying civilizations if the split occurred suddenly.

Volcanoes

Science writer Fred Warshofsky asks in his book *Doomsday: The Science of Catastrophe*, "Must all major geologic changes occur slowly," or is there something "that would speed the drift of continents . . . in a sudden, convulsive lurch?" He believes there is. Studies of Mars may shed light on the question. He writes, "Circular scars that surround [the] poles [on Mars] are considered evidence of radical movements by the poles." These scars may be volcanoes, which have also played a major role in shaping the surface of the earth.

While geologists acknowledge that volcanoes could have triggered continental drift in the past, most do not believe volcanic activity is a major factor today. But Warshofsky observes, "That is precisely the picture being drawn from cores pulled

Olympus Mons (mountain) is the largest volcano on Mars. It dwarfs Hawaii's Mauna Loa, earth's largest volcano.

In 1980, Mount St. Helens in Washington state erupted with devastating force. Scientists disagree on whether volcanoes could destroy the world.

from deep beneath the sea." Geologists are trying to learn more about the development of the earth by drilling holes deep into its core and pulling out samples of its layers. These samples, or cores, show that volcanoes played a major role in the formation of the earth's surface.

"These cores," says Warshofsky, are "built for the most part of sedimentary mud, coral skeletons and segments of volcanic ash." They indicate that major volcanic eruptions once took place, shaking "the earth to its foundations." These produced shudders that sent continents rocking over the earth "like so many corks bouncing on the waves." Warshofsky says that evidence taken from 320 cores from various ocean sites indicates that much volcanic activity occurred in the last two million years. He concludes that erupting volcanoes accompanied by earthquakes could change the face of the earth.

Will earth changes in the form of volcanoes send the earth reeling? At this point, scientists do not agree on the answer. Some, in fact, predict an even more dramatic end to the world as we know it—a pole shift.

Pole Shift—Fact or Fantasy?

The idea of a pole shift—the earth flipping over, with the North Pole becoming the South Pole and vice versa—is not new. In his book *The Bear Tribe's Self-Reliance Book*, Sun Bear recounts a Hopi myth about pole shift:

> And so, once again, Sotukuang was ordered to destroy the world. This time he ordered the Twins, Poquanghoya and Palongawhoya, to leave their stations at the North and South Poles and let the world be destroyed. . . . After the Twins left their stations, the world's stability was removed and so it flipped end over end and everything on it was destroyed by ice.

Sun Bear thinks this myth is evidence that the earth's poles shifted in the past. If the poles were to shift, the earth would suffer worldwide destruction from awesome tidal waves, hurricanes with winds of hundreds of miles per hour, volcanoes, earthquakes, and instant, extreme climate changes. Ruth Montgomery believes such a shift could happen. She claims her supernatural sources show her that previous shifts occurred in 50,000 B.C. and 150,000 B.C. She says an imbalance of the earth on its axis caused the shifts. The earth became lopsided from snow and ice that had built up at the poles.

Science writer Bill Lawren writes in *Psychology Today* that Montgomery "foresees a cosmic [universal] ecodisaster in which the North and South poles suddenly change places, . . . turning the surface of the planet inside out and in general wreaking havoc on real-estate values."

Controversial Evidence

Others disagree with Montgomery's scenario. John White says there is no real evidence that previous shifts occurred: "From a scientific perspective,

Psychic Ruth Montgomery claims that a supernatural source revealed to her a coming shift in the earth's poles—an event that would likely end the world.

pole shifts are nothing to worry about because there is almost no scientific basis to the concept."

Earth scientist John Gribbin points out one problem with this theory—the idea that a buildup of ice at the poles will unbalance the earth and make it topple. Gribbin writes, "Doomsayers make such forecasts in spite of the fact that the average ice cover has actually decreased during the present century." Without such a buildup, a shift is unlikely. Moreover, he claims, far greater quantities of ice existed on the poles during the last ice age without creating a shift.

Those who believe a major pole shift may occur point to the frozen Stone Age woolly mammoths found in Siberia and Alaska as key pieces of evidence for a shift. They say the perfect preservation of the mammoths suggests they died quickly and were frozen. A pole shift could have created a drastic climate change that caused the animals to freeze.

On the other hand, Daniel Cohen is one of many experts who claim that frozen mammoths can be easily explained without considering a pole shift as

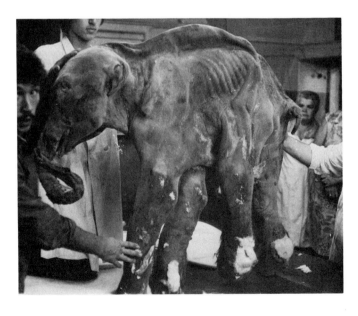

Frozen ten thousand years ago in Siberia, this perfectly preserved baby woolly mammoth carcass is examined by scientists. Some people believe that such "quick frozen" specimens indicate a past shift in the North and South poles.

the cause. The animals could have fallen into deep crevasses and been preserved in permafrost, a permanently frozen layer found in frigid regions. Cohen explains:

> Quickly, the dead mammoths would become covered with mud and snow from above. The mud would freeze, and the carcasses would be securely embedded in the permafrost. . . . No overnight catastrophic deep freezes need be brought in to account for the frozen mammoths. Besides, both the number and state of preservation of the mammoths is usually exaggerated by those who like to see mysteries where there are none.

In other words, mammoths could have died from freak accidents like falling into icy ravines and frozen lakes. Cohen also points out that arctic winds are sufficient to freeze a mammoth.

Outworn Ideas

Gribbin believes the pole-shift theories are based on outworn ideas. Instead, he suggests, continental drift might have caused the unusual phenomena that are now attributed to pole shifts. As the continents drift slowly over the globe, they could occasionally pass over polar regions and the tropics. Gribbin writes:

> Just as the scars of ancient glaciers are found in Brazil and Africa, so deposits of coal, the remains of long-gone tropical jungles, are found in Antarctica. Pole-shifters say that millions of years ago the tropics must have been "in Antarctica" and the north pole "in Brazil." Continental-drift theory says that, rather, long ago Antarctica was in the tropics, and has since drifted slowly to its present position.

The theory further says that Brazil at some time in the past drifted over the North Pole. Gribbin points out that drift could happen at a rate of a few centimeters per year, "not the sudden flipping over of the Earth end for end."

Some believe a new ice age could mean the end of the world as we know it, even without a pole shift. California talk show host Mobius Rex is one who predicts the earth will undergo another ice age soon. Some scientists agree. Sir Fred Hoyle, in his book *Ice: The Ultimate Human Catastrophe*, argues that an ice age could come within a decade. If it does, glaciers of ice will cover most of Great Britain as well as the northern United States and Europe.

Ice Age Cycles

John Gribbin says that for the past million years, the earth has gone through regular climate cycles. It undergoes a period of intense cold for 100,000 years, which is followed by a slight warming, called an interglacial period, for some 10,000 years. Then, the cold period returns. The earth is presently in an interglacial period.

Yugoslav earth scientist Milatin Milankovitch developed the idea of how ice ages come and go. Gribbin says, "The Milankovitch Model indicates very clearly that as the centuries go by and summers become cooler and cooler, at some point a critical balance [between cooling and warming] is passed. Then, just one very severe winter . . . could provide so much snowfall that great white sheets of snow would persist throughout the following cool summer." The snow would reflect the sun's heat back into the atmosphere, keeping the earth refrigerated. The planet would plunge into a new ice age in a matter of years. "For the record . . . a new full ice age is due. If you want to worry about the threat of ice, it is a realistic threat. The 'next' ice age could indeed come in our lifetimes, without the Earth toppling over in space," Gribbin says.

Some scientists say the last ice age ended less than ten thousand years ago and lasted twenty thousand years. According to Fred Warshofsky, the debate centers around *when* a new ice age will start,

not *if*. "Why this sudden spate of doom and gloom?" asks Warshofsky. "Because the climate has been changing and with frightening rapidity."

One of the reasons the planet's climate is changing, according to many scientists, is because of people's mismanagement of the environment. This, along with other human-caused problems, could wreak havoc on the world.

Great mountains of ice dominate the polar regions of earth. Some scientists predict the arrival of a new ice age very soon. Glaciers and icebergs would then cover much of the earth, ending the world as we know it.

Five

Are People Creating Their Own Doomsday?

(Opposite page) This 1990 photo of the cracked, dry bottom of Santa Barbara's Gibraltar Reservoir is clear evidence that California suffered a severe drought. Unusual weather events have occurred in recent years throughout the world. Are they signs that doomsday looms as a punishment for humanity's ecological sins?

During the end of the 1980s and beginning of the 1990s, California suffered a severe drought. Drought also occurred in other vast areas of North America, wiping out crops, dramatically reducing the flow of water in rivers, and leading to raging forest fires that swept over millions of acres in the West. Record-setting spring and summer temperatures and heat waves occurred throughout the United States. In 1988, the United States had its driest year in nearly a century.

Weird Weather

According to geologist and writer Jon Erickson in *Greenhouse Earth*, such unusual weather has been occurring around the globe over the last two decades. Australia had its worst drought in more than 100 years in 1983. In 1983 and 1984, drought in Africa was the worst in 150 years, leaving millions of people dead or dying of starvation and disease. At the same time, the worst flooding of the century hit Ecuador, northern Peru, Brazil, Paraguay, and Argentina. In the late 1980s, the Sahara Desert had four inches of snowfall—a phenomenon never before recorded. In February 1989, unusual hurricane winds hit Ireland and northern England, and in March 1989, ocean temperatures

near the Philippines were abnormally high.

Some scientists, noting these events, believe the cause may be people. Increased pollution is causing the earth's surface and atmosphere to become warmer, through a process known as the greenhouse effect. In his book *Future Weather and the Greenhouse Effect*, John Gribbin explains: "By burning fossil fuel (oil and, especially, coal), by slash-and-burn agriculture, and by tearing down tropical rainforest, [people are] producing a rapid buildup of carbon dioxide in the atmosphere." Carbon dioxide is released during the burning of fuels or wood. Gribbin continues, "This [layer of carbon dioxide pollution] . . . acts as a blanket around the Earth, trapping heat that would otherwise radiate away into space, and causing the surface of the planet to

Smoke from a Brazilian farmer's slash-and-burn clearing method chokes the primeval rain forest of the Amazon Basin. Rain forest destruction occurs at an alarming rate, possibly threatening the well-being of the whole planet.

warm up." Even a modest warming due to the greenhouse effect would change temperatures and rainfall around the globe. This, in turn, would disrupt worldwide agricultural practices.

Global warming could raise sea levels, thereby increasing evaporation and rain and also increasing the global cloud cover. This would alter the climate across the planet. Arctic ice, for example, could melt, devastating arctic habitats and further changing the world's weather and climate. Agricultural outputs could be drastically reduced as a result. People would starve all over the world.

Increased Burning Leads to Increased Carbon Dioxide

Since the beginning of the Industrial Revolution in the nineteenth century, people have been burning fossil fuels at ever-increasing rates. This burning releases carbon dioxide into the atmosphere. Normally, trees and other plants use up much of this carbon dioxide and, in turn, release fresh oxygen into the air. But excessive burning of these fuels combined with wholesale clearing of forests has boosted carbon dioxide levels by 25 percent since the beginning of the industrial era.

Scientists estimate that the burning of fossil fuels spews 5.4 billion tons of carbon dioxide into the atmosphere each year. Deforestation, or the cutting down of forests, adds 1 to 2.6 billion more tons. At this rate, scientists think carbon dioxide levels could raise the planet's temperature by three to nine degrees Fahrenheit by around the year 2050. Meteorological statistics support this theory. For example, the meteorological office of the United Kingdom reported in 1989 that the six warmest years of the century occurred in the 1980s.

Other pollutants may also be contributing to the greenhouse effect. These include methane, which is produced, for example, by natural gas, rotting garbage, and bacteria found in cattle and termites;

An Illinois farmer in despair over his corn crop, shriveled by the 1988 drought. The exceedingly hot, dry summer that year forced the world to consider the reality of global warming.

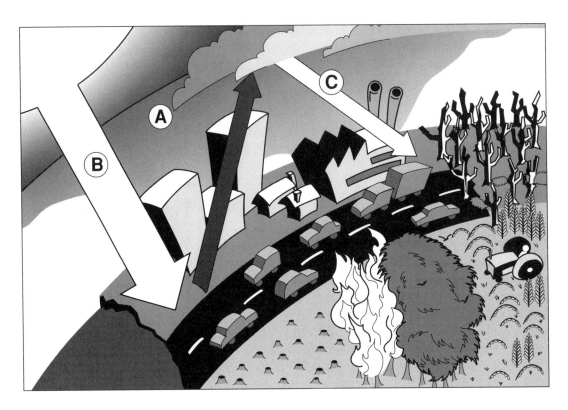

Many human activities, including deforestation, release carbon dioxide and other pollutants into the atmosphere where they form a barrier (A). Sunlight (B) is able to penetrate this barrier to warm the earth. The sun's heat, however, is unable to escape back into the atmosphere and instead comes back to earth (C), causing global warming.

nitrous oxide, which is produced largely by auto exhaust and power plants; and CFCs (chlorofluorocarbons), which come from air conditioners and aerosols, among other sources. CFCs are powerful gases that destroy the ozone layer in the upper atmosphere. Ozone prevents dangerous ultraviolet (UV) light from entering the atmosphere. UV light can cause blindness and skin cancer.

Dean Edwin Abrahamson is professor of public affairs at the University of Minnesota. In *The Challenge of Global Warming*, he writes that the situation is serious: "It is now clearly within our power . . . to alter the planet . . . within a few decades by destroying the earth's life-support systems and radically changing climate by contamination of the air and water." He thinks the consequences will be catastrophic if pollution is not stopped. Climatic change would be irreversible, causing major upheavals ecologically, economically, and socially.

Topsy-Turvy Weather Changes

Other scientists agree that the weather will grow worse. Cliff Harris, a Canadian climatologist (someone who studies the climate), says, "Things, weatherwise, are becoming increasingly berserk on a global basis. The current worldwide cycle of topsy-turvy temperatures and record-breaking storms will get a lot worse before things start to improve." Harris predicts that the last fifty years of the twentieth century will prove to have been the most extreme in hundreds of years.

Scientists at Woods Hole Research Center in Massachusetts agree that the climate is changing in unusual ways. Their studies show that climatic zones are shifting, glaciers and the polar ice caps are melting, and sea levels are rising. As sea levels rise, they will flood coastal cities and harbors, erode beaches and cliffs, bring salt water into drinking water supplies, and destroy coastal wetlands. Since most of the world's population lives in coastal areas, this could be a huge disaster. The U.S. Environ-

In Key West, Florida, federal inspectors check a mountain of garbage for hazardous materials before deciding to accept or reject it for a local dump. The problem of waste disposal has become unmanageable in some heavily populated regions.

Air quality in major urban areas like Los Angeles has reached crisis proportions. Besides threatening the health of everything that breathes, air pollution adds to global warming.

mental Protection Agency says there could be an eventual two- to seven-foot rise in the ocean level along the coasts of the United States.

James Hansen, director of NASA's Goddard Institute for Space Studies, agrees that freak global weather will continue. For example, he believes that by the year 2000, the frequency of days per year with temperatures exceeding 110°F in Dallas will increase by nineteen—from the present fifty-nine days per year to seventy-eight.

Wallace S. Broeker, a professor of geochemistry, argues in *The Challenge of Global Warming* that what is going on is unacceptable. He believes humanity's self-indulgence, its persistence in using manufacturing methods that emit carbon dioxide and other harmful gases, its dependence on the automobile, and other destructive habits will ultimately result in a world changed dramatically for the worse. "The inhabitants of planet Earth are quietly conducting a gigantic environmental experiment. So vast and so sweeping will be its impacts that, were it brought before any responsible council for approval, it would be firmly rejected as having potentially dangerous consequences," Broeker says.

Other scientists think the gloomy predictions of scientists like Broeker and Hansen are questionable. Some scientists do not even believe the greenhouse effect is real.

Is There a Greenhouse Effect?

Geologist and writer Jon Erickson, in his book *Greenhouse Earth*, points out that the greenhouse effect has not yet been proved. He states:

> The climate variability . . . is such that the strange weather can still be a reflection of natural variation. As yet, no sign of climate change has occurred that can be unquestionably blamed on the greenhouse effect. There might be unknown . . . factors that can cancel out or at least lessen the greenhouse effect. Scientists have yet to determine where all the carbon dioxide is going.

Only half of emitted carbon dioxide has been found in the oceans or in the atmosphere. "It must also be kept in mind that the climate is always changing," Erickson says. The earth goes through cycles of warm and cold. According to Erickson, if temperatures continue to rise in the 1990s, this could help prove that greenhouse warming is occurring.

"Few people today doubt that history is moving toward some sort of climactic catastrophe."

Hal Lindsey, *The Rapture*

"It is not the entire Earth . . . that passes through the end-time cataclysms so lovingly described by the pre-millennialists. Rather it is the individual consciousness, the individual ego of the spiritually undeveloped person."

Martin Levin, *Utne Reader*, March/April 1990

With the help of a United Nations agency, Paraguayan farmers plant new trees in an attempt to reverse the deforestation of their country.

In *Greenhouse Glasnost*, Carl Sagan writes, "Some scientists think the chance of a massive agricultural disaster from greenhouse warming by 2050 is low—perhaps only 10 percent." But Sagan himself thinks a future disaster is a possibility unless people take steps to avert it. Not everyone agrees. Some analysts claim it is impossible or undesirable to limit climatic change. They say instead that societies can cope with change through adaptation. But Dean Abrahamson states that this depends upon "how rapidly the climate is changing." If it changes too fast, adaptations cannot be made. It would take time to build dams and dikes, for instance, to keep up with any significant changes in the water supply. Adaptation is not a feasible solution, he suggests. "The time required for major changes in technological systems varies between 20 and 50 years and is probably between 30 and 50 for water projects."

Reversing Global Warming

How can global warming be stopped? Abrahamson suggests that three steps are essential. First, we must reduce greenhouse gases (carbon dioxide and

CFCs) until the amount produced can be removed by natural processes. Second, we must increase nature's power to remove these harmful gases from the atmosphere. Trees, for example, can absorb carbon dioxide. Therefore, a reforestation strategy must be planned. Third, we must find a way to cool the globe.

Ecologist Barry Commoner, in his book *Making Peace with the Planet*, suggests that even if global warming never becomes so severe as to cause a catastrophe,

> already human activity has profoundly altered global conditions. . . . Everywhere in the world, there is now radioactivity that was not there before, the dangerous residue of nuclear explosions and the nuclear power industry; noxious fumes of smog blanket every major city; carcinogenic [cancer-causing] . . . pesticides have been detected in mothers' milk all over the world; great forests have been cut down, destroying ecological niches and their resident species.

According to Commoner and other ecologists, ecocide—the destruction of the earth's ecology—is a reality and is slowly killing the world. They ur-

Day by day, the filth generated by human industry adds to the burden carried by the earth's ecosystems. Environmentalists warn of inevitable catastrophe if pollution is not halted soon.

An intercontinental ballistic missile emerges ominously from a cloud of smoke as it lifts off from its underground silo. The missile is one of thousands intended to carry nuclear warheads to targets all over the world. A nuclear holocaust is one very real end-of-the-world scenario.

gently stress that environmental problems must be addressed at once or the world as we know it will die.

Will the World End Through Nuclear War?

If ecocide does not ruin the planet, perhaps nuclear war will. Nostradamus, the sixteenth-century prophet, predicted a disaster "enclosed in containers, launched from a fleet of ships, in a single night it transforms a city to dust and vapor." Erika Chatham and other modern interpreters of Nostradamus say this verse predicts the catastrophe of nuclear war. Even Dick Teresi and Judith Hooper, who are skeptical of other doomsday scenarios, believe nuclear war could happen. They write in *Omni* magazine, "Our only hope is to count on the corruption of the defense industry and the ineptitude of the military: Maybe none of the missiles or warheads will actually work."

But the missiles do work. After the United States dropped atomic bombs on Japan in 1945, the Soviet Union developed its own bombs. The two countries plunged into an arms buildup that frequently threatened to break out into a nuclear war. Although the collapse of the Soviet Union ended the Cold War in 1989, neither country has significantly disarmed itself. In addition, several industrial nations possess nuclear weapons and so do smaller nations, including, some suspect, politically volatile ones. The end of the Cold War did not, unfortunately, end the threat of nuclear war.

Daniel Cohen points out that even if no nation deliberately starts such a war, it is possible for a nuclear war to break out accidentally. Although "the various . . . missile systems are highly automated, and we are assured that a catastrophic mistake is 'impossible,' even a falling asteroid could trigger launch systems," he says.

Not only do modern nuclear weapons make the bombs that were dropped on Japan look like toys but the United States by itself still has enough warheads to destroy every major city with a population of more than 100,000 in the Commonwealth of Independent States thirty-six times over.

In October 1983, a group of scientists met for a conference about the likely state of the world after a nuclear war. Their studies seemed to confirm the unthinkable—a nuclear war could spell final doom for the planet and for people. On the basis of computer-simulated war studies, they predicted that a nuclear war would cause global extinction. The study, called TTAPS after the initials of the five scientists who wrote the report, predicts that such a war would cause "nuclear winter," an environmental catastrophe in which the world would suffer long-lasting and devastating artificial winter.

Nuclear Winter

When initial nuclear attacks destroy all the major cities in the Northern Hemisphere, up to 1.1 billion deaths could occur outright, according to TTAPS. An additional 1.1 billion casualties could result within a short period of time. Says Paul R. Ehrlich in the book *The Cold and the Dark*:

> As many people *as existed on the planet when our nation was founded* would be vaporized, disintegrated, mashed, pulped, and smeared over the landscape by the explosive force of the bombs. . . . Virtually all cities—which are the political, industrial, transport, financial, communications, and cultural centers of societies—would simply cease to exist. Much of humanity's know-how would disappear along with them. . . . The fates of the 2-3 billion people who are not killed immediately . . . might in many ways be worse.

They would suffer freezing temperatures, darkness, starvation, disease, and radiation sickness.

Huge fire storms generated by the explosions would sweep across the attack area. People in shel-

"Is there anything on or in the earth itself that is likely to bring about the end of people? The answer is probably no."

Daniel Cohen, *Waiting for the Apocalypse*

"At present we are heading for extinction and who will shed tears for us? Who regrets the dinosaur?"

Nobel Prize-winning chemist Albert Szent-Györgyi

ters would be burned or smothered. The temperature on the ground would be in the thousands of degrees. Clouds of poisonous gases would rise and cover the cities.

According to science writer Gene B. Williams in *Nuclear War, Nuclear Winter*, billions of tons of dust, soot, and ash "would be tossed into the atmosphere, accompanied by smoke" and fumes. This would block out the sunlight. Temperatures would quickly drop to freezing and below. Darkness would reign for twenty-four hours a day and could last for months or a year. Survivors would not be able to grow food under these conditions. The entire climate of the planet would change. Global radioactive fallout would drastically affect all life.

Williams explains, "Within a couple of days, the cold begins to set in. The sun is blotted out. Even those areas that were far from the blasts are affected. The plants begin to freeze and die. You almost wish that the cities and forests were still burning, just for some warmth."

Millions more people would die from cold and starvation. After nine months, the sun would occasionally come out. But the land would be wasted and barren. There would be no one to bury the billions of dead and frozen people. Constant danger of severe radiation contamination would be constant for five years or so. According to Carl Sagan, survivors would also suffer "social disruption; the unavailability of electricity, fuel, transportation, food deliveries, communications, and other civil service; the absence of medical care; the decline in sanitation measures; rampant disease and severe [mental] disorders would doubtless claim . . . further victims."

"No Sanctuaries from Nuclear War"

In the foreword to *The Cold and the Dark*, the late physician Lewis Thomas remarks, "There is no nation on Earth free of the jeopardy of destruction if

Dr. Lewis Thomas, former dean of the Yale University School of Medicine, warns U.S. leaders of the chilling consequences of a nuclear exchange.

a nuclear exchange occurs. The elaborate, coherent, beautifully organized ecosystem of the Earth—what some people call the biosphere and others refer to as nature—will have been dealt a mortal or near-mortal blow." Carl Sagan echoes this idea: "There are no sanctuaries from nuclear war anywhere on Earth."

TTAPS predicted that nuclear winter would occur after even a minor nuclear exchange.

Are the TTAPS scientists right? Would a nuclear war be utterly devastating? Biologist David Ehrenfeld writes in an article in *The Last Extinction* that Sagan and the others are probably right about nuclear winter. However, he says, "There may be some scientific variable they have overlooked, which . . . would change the results."

Although some scientists do not believe nuclear winter would happen, most do believe it is very

Cornell scientist Carl Sagan explains to a congressional committee the ecological disaster that would result from a nuclear war. The drawing on the right maps a hypothetical nuclear exchange of one hundred missiles.

Hungry Ethiopians await the arrival of food relief during one of many famines they endured in the 1980s. Some experts believe that overpopulation threatens the future of human life on earth.

possible, and they believe the TTAPS model presents a realistic picture of its effects. Nuclear war, say most scientists, would be a real doomsday.

Overpopulation—Will People Survive Overcrowding?

Overpopulation is another way some experts believe people could cause doomsday.

According to Sun Bear, an estimated sixty million people worldwide starved to death in 1990. In poor countries such as India and many African nations, forty thousand babies die every day. Some people believe that these deaths are the result of overpopulation—too many people.

The world's population has been growing steadily over the last several decades. In 1968, the global population was 3.5 billion people. In 1990, it was around 5.3 billion. Every hour, 11,000 people are born, or 95 million a year. Population experts Paul and Anne Ehrlich first raised the alarm about overpopulation in their 1971 book *The Population Bomb*. In 1990, they published a new version of the book, *The Population Explosion*, in which they claimed that the dangers they described nearly twenty years before remained the same, in spite of the efforts made by groups such as Zero Population Growth to educate the public about this issue.

The Ehrlichs say overpopulation leads to famine, more pollution, greater consumption of resources, increased crowding, higher rates of crime, and increased violence. The increased use of petroleum, for example, results in air pollution, which causes global warming and affects weather patterns. Changing weather patterns disrupt agricultural practices, leading to food shortages and thus to hunger and starvation.

In order to feed and provide income for a burgeoning population, this section of the South American rain forest has been cleared to create pasture for cattle. Overpopulation, rain forest destruction, and poor economies threaten an ever-increasing number of nations.

As part of an environmental project, a volunteer catalogs debris washed up on a Chicago beach. Humans may finally destroy the world by choking it with waste.

Furthermore, overpopulation leads to the expansion and intensification of agriculture, which damages soil and depletes groundwater reserves. Communities of plants, animals, and microorganisms vanish as people take over more of the planet's surface either through agriculture or development.

More people in developed nations leads to the overconsumption of other resources as well. Deforestation of rain forests, for example, results from the world's increasing demand for cheap beef. In much of Central America, forests have been cut and converted to pastures for cattle. After a few years, the depleted pastures are abandoned and other forests are cut down for new pastures.

Overpopulation, according to the Ehrlichs, contributes to crime and violence. Large, crowded cities lack community feeling, and the resulting alienation allows people to prey upon one another. Crime and violence are also tied to unemployment rates, lack of education, racial prejudice, and stress, all of which are correlated to population size, they claim.

The Ehrlichs ask, "What do we gain by playing environmental roulette," by allowing our popula-

Stacks of logs await processing at a lumber mill. Wealthy nations' desire for exotic tropical hardwoods encourages rain forest nations to cut down too many trees. Trees form the base of the rain forest ecosystem without which the planet may not survive.

A poor Brazilian farmer searches the skies for rain to revive his drooping crop. Some believe that droughts, famines, and wars herald the approach of doomsday.

tions to continue to grow beyond the breaking point? "We've played, and now we're starting to pay. The alarm has been sounded repeatedly, but society has turned a deaf ear. *Meanwhile, a largely prospective disaster has turned into the real thing. . . .* Hunger is rife and the prospects of famine and plague even more imminent," they say.

"If humanity fails to act, *nature may end the population explosion for us*—in very unpleasant ways—well before the 10 billion population mark is reached," according to the Ehrlichs. They believe the world in the 1990s will be confronted by more urgent environmental problems, especially global warming, "a problem caused in large part by population growth and overpopulation." Population growth in already overcrowded nations will make it very difficult to slow greenhouse warming or to stop or reverse it, they claim. It would be like trying

"The very real possibility that man might completely destroy himself became apparent on August 6, 1945, when a U.S. bomber dropped an atomic bomb on the Japanese city of Hiroshima."

Daniel Cohen, *Waiting for the Apocalypse*

"Most of the biblical passages that supposedly presage World War III really concern ancient politics, according to mainstream theologians."

Dick Teresi and Judith Hooper, *Omni*, January 1990

to slow down a supertanker. Such an effort takes time because of the momentum of the ship. The larger the population and the more it uses technologies that contribute to global warming, the harder it will be to reverse this dangerous trend. "We shouldn't delude ourselves; the population explosion will come to an end before very long." In other words, they say, nature will take the upper hand and reduce the population through famine, disease, epidemics, and storms. "Crop failures due to global warming might result in the premature deaths of a billion or more people in the next few decades," say the Ehrlichs.

They urge action to stop and reverse overpopulation. The birthrate should be lowered to less than the death rate right away, they say. If this is not done, the end of civilization could come within a few decades. The result of continued population growth will be more droughts, more damaged and failed crops, more dying forests, more smog, more international crime, and more sewage, they argue.

Daniel Cohen agrees the future will be dim without population control. He points out that there is increasing concern that "the end of the world might be brought about by . . . pollution. We are currently poisoning ourselves, our air, and water at a horrifying rate. As the population rises, the need for fresh air and water also rises. So too do the demands for power and manufactured goods which produce the production in the first place. Something has to give."

A Modern Mass Extinction?

Moreover, according to the Ehrlichs, overpopulation is dooming plants and animals worldwide. They state, "The planet's plants, animals, and microorganisms are now threatened with a colossal extinction epidemic. It may prove to be a crisis even more severe than the actual episode that ended the reign of dinosaurs some 65 million years ago."

They and other scientists claim the earth is losing its biodiversity, or its numerous forms of life. This would be a disaster, they argue. People have survived by using plants and animals for food, clothing, and industrial purposes. They have also used nature to obtain ingredients for medicines. Nature contains a "genetic library," a vast source of genes that produce diverse forms of life. The Ehrlichs point out that people have barely begun to use the potential of nature to benefit the world. So far, for example, people have bred food crops from just a few species of the grasses available in the genetic library. When plants and animals become extinct, their potential usefulness is lost forever. Humanity loses opportunities for new foods, medicines, and industrial materials.

Biodiversity is being lost through industrialization and urbanization. It is also being lost through

Rain forests (darkly shaded area) cover a relatively small area of the planet's surface but play an indispensable role in its preservation.

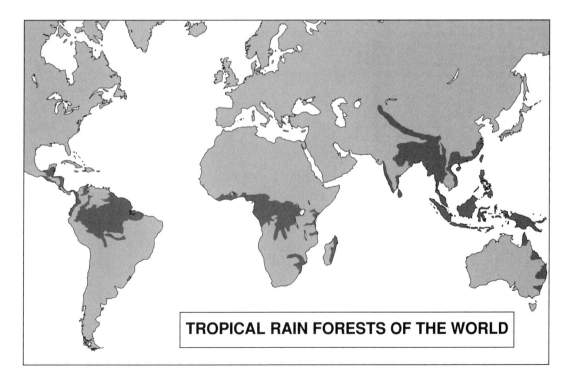

TROPICAL RAIN FORESTS OF THE WORLD

A young boy passes in front of a burning rain forest in the Amazon region. The Amazon fires clear away brush for pastures and crops. The expansion of agriculture and cattle raising is a serious threat to the survival of the rain forest.

the conversion of wilderness into farmland. The earth is losing tropical forests, for example, at a rate of at least 200,000 square kilometers a year. This results from the logging and clearing of forests for agriculture and cattle raising.

Biologist David Ehrenfeld supports the Ehrlichs' assertions. He says one-fourth of all medicines come from tropical plants. "In spite of this, tropical species are being driven into extinction much faster than they can be tested for medical use," he says.

The Value of Biodiversity

The loss of biodiversity also threatens strains of important crops. Scientists have long crossbred different strains of similar plants to increase hardiness and resistance to insects and disease. Rare and wild relatives of crops serve as sources of new genes that help crops fight their natural and human-caused enemies. Paul Ehrlich states:

> New wheat strains resistant to rust fungi have a life expectancy of only about five years in the northwestern United States. Then a new variety of fungus evolves that can attack the strain, and a new crop strain that is resistant to the rust must be ready for planting. But creation of the new strain is possible only if the requisite genes are available.

A varied genetic pool is needed to draw from as agricultural and environmental conditions change. The loss of biodiversity could be a disaster in terms of feeding people. According to the Ehrlichs, only "a few of the more than a quarter-million kinds of plants that exist have been investigated for their potential as crops." The destruction of tropical forests could eliminate the possibilities of creating new strains of plants and crops.

According to Fred Warshofsky:

> It appears that no species is exempt from sudden extinction at the hands of man. The largest creatures left on earth, the giant blue whales, face almost immediate extinction. . . . There are more than 100 species of whale, and they are fast being hunted into extinction by greedy, violent men. . . . Our attack is aimed not only at the largest of the earth's creatures, but at all of them, even the smallest. . . . In March 1975 the Department of the Interior announced that of the 700 kinds of butterflies in the United States, it was placing 41 on its list of endangered species.

People do not fully understand that all lifeforms are interdependent, says Warshofsky. By destroying other creatures, people could end up destroying themselves. "Imagine the horror, shock, and disbelief when we must enter upon the endangered species list" people themselves, he suggests.

"What is truly significant is that we have reached a point where the destruction of mankind and the earth is now not only technologically possible, but statistically probable."

Fred Warshofsky, *Doomsday: The Science of Catastrophe*

"[It is] better to make our own futures than sit around and wait for them to happen."

Charles J. Cazeau, *The Skeptical Inquirer*, Winter 1990

Scientists believe less than two million species of plants and animals remain on earth. Some predict the extinction rate will increase dramatically. In 1979, about one hundred species a year became extinct; by the year 2000, the rate could be as high as forty thousand annually.

Biologist Les Kaufman, however, has a more optimistic view. He writes in *The Last Extinction* that no one really knows how bad extinction is. He claims there is no current data, "especially on organisms yet to be discovered." The extinction rate could be worse than believed, or it could be better. It might be only half of what has been projected. Still, half of forty thousand is a lot of extinctions.

Some people claim extinction is a normal process and nothing to worry about. But David Ehrenfeld compares the modern extinction rate among

A right whale, a member of an endangered species, surfaces for a breath of air. Human activity has accounted for the demise of uncounted species of plants and animals on earth.

most groups of mammals with the rate from the late Pleistocene period. He calculated that in 1970, the rate was one thousand times greater. Today, he suspects, it is even worse.

A large proportion of the world's species live in tropical rain forests in the Southern Hemisphere. Florida State University ecologist David Simberloff has estimated that when only one-third of the world's tropical forests are left, which ecologists estimate will happen in two to three decades, as many as 625,000 species will be extinct. That is nearly one-half of all the 1.7 million species of plants and animals that have been identified so far on earth. Ehrenfeld says, "Other estimates are considerably higher." Every day, species become extinct due to the activities of people—deforestation, reduction of habitat, and pollution. He thinks that human beings will probably cause an even greater disaster for life on this planet than the one sixty-five million years ago that destroyed the dinosaurs and numerous other species.

Will people create their own doomsday? If some of the scientists are right, perhaps so. As Les Kaufman warns in *The Last Extinction*, "If other species can disappear so quickly, regardless of their strengths and weaknesses, so can we."

Epilogue

The 1990s—The Last Decade?

Will the world end in the 1990s? Will it end in 1999 as Nostradamus predicted? Doomsday writer Charles Berlitz remarks, "Some of the most fearful prophecies from the past are alarmingly close in content and in time location to today's pessimistic scientific forecasts." He adds, "Prophecies of the world's end by fire, ice, water, or explosion, although made in different ages and in different cultures during the past 6,000 years, seem to agree that the age of doom is fairly close at hand."

Berlitz believes three possible and close dangers threaten the world at present. One is the protective reaction of the earth, in the form of earth changes, against humanity's excesses. He says this possibility is "imaginable but unlikely." Another is a cosmic catastrophe that will destroy the earth. He says this is "possible but far from certain." Finally, he says, is the possibility of humanity's self-destruction through nuclear war. This danger, he says, is "fairly possible."

Perhaps the most interesting point regarding doomsday is that prophecies and science seem to agree that if things continue as they are, catastrophe is around the corner. It can be averted, however, if people take steps, especially environmentally. But John White remarks in *The Meeting of Science and Spirit* that people need not dwell on the future "as a

source of fear and destruction. Our primary task as citizens of Earth," he says, "is to attune ourselves spiritually with Life—with the processes of the planet and the cosmos—and thereby understand that . . . we are being given an occasion to grow, to evolve." He believes there is still time to solve our problems.

For Further Exploration

William A. Alnor, *Soothsayers of the Second Advent.* Old Tappan, NJ: Fleming H. Revell, 1989.

Frank Close, *Apocalypse When?* New York: William Morrow, 1988.

Daniel Cohen, *Waiting for the Apocalypse.* New York: Prometheus Books, 1983.

National Geographic Society, *The Powers of Nature.* Washington, DC: National Geographic Society, 1978.

Sun Bear, *Black Dawn, Bright Sky.* Spokane, WA: Bear Tribe Publishing, 1990.

Fred Warshofsky, *Doomsday: The Science of Catastrophe.* New York: Reader's Digest Press, 1977.

Works Consulted

Dean Edwin Abrahamson, ed., *The Challenge of Global Warming*. Washington, DC: Island Press, 1989.

Isaac Asimov, *A Choice of Catastrophes*. New York: Simon & Schuster, 1979.

Charles Berlitz, *Doomsday: 1999 A.D.* Garden City, NY: Doubleday, 1981.

Page Bryant, *The Earth Changes Survival Handbook*. Santa Fe, NM: Sun Publishing Company, 1983.

Nigel Calder, *The Comet Is Coming*. New York: Viking Press, 1980.

Clark R. Chapman and David Morrison, *Cosmic Catastrophes*. New York: Plenum Press, 1989.

Victor Clube and Bill Napier, *The Cosmic Winter*. Oxford, England: Basil Blackwell, 1990.

Barry Commoner, *Making Peace with the Planet*. New York: Pantheon Books, 1990.

Peter Roche de Coppens, *Apocalypse Now*. St. Paul, MN: Llewellyn Publications, 1988.

Martin Ebon, *Prophecy in Our Time*. New York: New American Library, 1968.

Paul R. Ehrlich and Anne H. Ehrlich, *The Population Explosion*. New York: Simon & Schuster, 1990.

Jon Erickson, *Greenhouse Earth*. Blue Ridge Summit, PA: Tab Books, 1990.

Leon Festinger, Henry W. Riecken, and Stanley Schacter, *When Prophecy Fails*. Minneapolis: University of Minnesota Press, 1956.

John Gribbin, *Future Weather and the Greenhouse Effect*. New York: Delacorte Press/Eleanor Friede, 1982.

John Gribbin and Stephen Plagemann, *Beyond the Jupiter Effect*. London: MacDonald, 1983.

T.A. Heppenheimer, *The Coming Quake*. New York: Random House/Times Books, 1988.

Fred Hoyle, *Ice: The Ultimate Human Catastrophe*. New York: Continuum, 1981.

Les Kaufman and Kenneth Mallory, eds., *The Last Extinction*. Cambridge, MA: MIT Press, 1986.

Hal Lindsey, *The Late Great Planet Earth*. New York: Bantam, 1970.

Hal Lindsey, *The Rapture*. New York: Bantam, 1983.

John Maddox, *The Doomsday Syndrome*. New York: McGraw-Hill, 1972.

Terrell J. Minger, ed., *Greenhouse Glasnost*. New York: The Ecco Press, 1990.

Ruth Montgomery, *Herald of the New Age*. Garden City, NY: Doubleday, 1986.

Richard Muller, *Nemesis, the Death Star*. New York: Weidenfeld & Nicolson, 1988.

Omni, January 1990.

Carl Sagan and Ann Druyan, *Comet*. New York: Random House, 1985.

Ted Schultz, ed., *The Fringes of Reason*. New York: Harmony Books, 1989.

William H. Stiebing Jr., *Ancient Astronauts, Cosmic Collisions*. New York: Prometheus Books, 1984.

Sun Bear, Wabun, and Nimimosha, *The Bear Tribe's Self-Reliance Book*. New York: Prentice House Press, 1988.

Utne Reader, March/April 1990.

Immanuel Velikovsky, *Worlds in Collision*. New York: Pocket Books, 1950.

David Wallechinsky, Amy Wallace, and Irving Wallace, *The Book of Predictions*. New York: William Morrow, 1980.

Jonathan Weiner, *Planet Earth*. New York: Bantam, 1986.

John White, *The Meeting of Science and Spirit*. New York: Paragon House, 1990.

John White, *Pole Shift*. Virginia Beach, VA: A.R.E. Press, 1988.

Gene B. Williams, *Nuclear War, Nuclear Winter*. New York: Franklin Watts, 1987.

Index

About the Author

Michael Arvey is a free-lance writer who has lived all over the United States. He has worked in a variety of occupations including meditation instructor, poet, and massage therapist. He has college degrees in communications, English, journalism, and creative writing. Arvey was press liaison for the 1988 Conference on World Affairs in Boulder, Colorado, where he makes his home. Currently he writes, edits, and teaches correspondence courses in creative writing. Michael Arvey has written several books in the Great Mysteries series including *ESP, UFOs,* and *Reincarnation.*

Picture Credits

Mary Ahrndt, 73 (top); American Meteorite Laboratory, 39; AP/Wide World Photos, 9, 18, 24, 26, 30, 32, 46, 74, 75, 81, 82, 83, 86, 89, 96 (top), 100; Courtesy Aurora University, 16, 17; Courtesy Bear Tribe Publishing, 63; The Bettmann Archive, 10, 14, 21, 35; Courtesy of the Archives, California Institute of Technology, 71; Supplied by Carolina Biological Supply, 79; Center for Coastal Studies, 102; Albrecht Durer, *The Apocalypse*, 22; Earthquake Info Bulletin 543/U.S. Geological Survey, 65; Food and Agriculture Organization of the United Nations, 96 (bottom), 97; The Granger Collection, New York, 12; Steven Gross/The University of Chicago, 50 (top); Benjamin Montag, 84; Artwork by Tom Miller © 1984 by the Science Museum of Virginia, 48; NASA, 38 (both), 40, 43, 44, 52, 105; National Library of Medicine, 11; Rainforest Action Network, 95; Reuters/Bettmann, 25 (bottom), 67; Smithsonian Institution, 47; United Nations, 88, 96 (bottom), 97; U.S. Air Force, 90; U.S. Geological Survey 585, 36; U.S. Geological Survey/Department of the Interior, 54, 55; U.S. Geological Survey/NASA, 73 (bottom); University of California at Berkeley, 51; U of M Rare Book Collection, 29; UPI/Bettmann, 25 (top), 27, 50 (bottom), 61, 62, 72, 76, 85, 92, 93, 94; Wallace, R.E. 194/U.S. Geological Survey, 69